Praise for the Innovative Leaders Guide to Transforming Organizations

This guide offers leaders a pragmatic set of tools to concurrently transform themselves and their organizations. Alignment is particularly important when transforming complex international organizations, and this book helps leaders align themselves, their organizational culture, and their systems to ensure success. The combination of theory and practice make this a must-read leadership book!

William I. Brustein, Ph.D., Vice Provost for Global Strategies and International Affairs, Professor of Sociology, Political Science, and History, The Ohio State University

■■■■■■■

This guide provides an essential blend of change leadership and individual leadership development tools necessary to successfully transform today's complex organizations. It is a must read!

Kate Terrell, Vice President, Human Resources Global Products Organization, Whirlpool Corporation

■■■■■■■

The process is compelling, the message is clear! This guide will give you a head start and improve your ability to lead transformational change.

Hugh Cathey, Principal, Columbus-Partners, LLC

■■■■■■■

Metcalf marries the art and science of change management into a playbook that maps a path to new levels of organizational performance. If you are betting big on transformative change, you'll find the insights in this guide will make you a master of that journey.

Ralph Spitzen, Director, Continuous Improvement, Worthington Steel

■■■■■■■

The guide reveals the importance of leadership development in facilitating complex organizational change. Its comprehensive models and processes help you develop as a leader even as you transform your organization. The end result: positive change for your organization, and personal growth for you.

Dan Mushalko, CEO WCBE, Board Member Friends of WCBE Public Radio

This is the most pragmatic change book I've ever read! As a leader implementing transformative change in my hospital, I found the tools and principles in the *Innovative Leaders Guide to Transforming Organizations* invaluable to our success.

Andy Manzur, President and CEO, Schuyler Hospital

■■■■■■■

Innovative Leaders Guide to Transforming Organizations is a unique and extraordinary contribution to understanding what it takes to lead complex change.

Beth Savage, Director, Financial Advisory Services, GBQ Consulting

■■■■■■■

Effective leadership and transformation skills are the main ingredients to create a recipe for success, and Metcalf offers great tools to effectively lead organizational transformation by melding authentic leadership with action.

Hal Krebs, CEO, Haladon Technologies, Inc.

■■■■■■■

This guide addresses the critical importance of the leader in transforming organizations. We live in a world that is blurred by the speed of change. The book provides a clear and comprehensive model for successful, results oriented leadership in an environment that is increasingly being defined by complex, rapid change."

Elyzabeth Holford, Executive Director, Equality Ohio

■■■■■■■

The complexity of organizational transformation requires a solid understanding of the art and science of leadership, operations, and transformation. This guide captures the essence of the transformation process and the art of the leader's thinking and shares it in a way that readers at all levels within the organization can understand and implement.

Mike Harris, President and CEO, Patina Solutions

■■■■■■■

The Innovative Leaders Guide to Transforming Organizations is extremely well done. It provides a clear process and gives examples of the tools necessary to successfully lead transformation within any organization.

Michael Linton, Retired CEO Adecco, CEO Staffing Leadership

INNOVATIVE
LEADERS GUIDE
TO TRANSFORMING
ORGANIZATIONS

Field-Tested Integrative Approaches to Developing Leaders,
Transforming Organizations, and Creating Sustainability

MAUREEN METCALF

FOREWORD BY CARLA PAONESSA • WORKBOOK SERIES EDITOR, MARK PALMER

First Published by
Integral Publishers
1418 N. Jefferson Ave.
Tucson, AZ 85712

Published in the United States with printing and
distribution in the United Kingdom, Australia,
and the European Union.

ISBN: 978-1-4675-2281-6

First Printing April 2013

Cover Design, Graphics and Layout by
Creative Spot - www.creativespot.com

Acknowledgments

This book represents the synthesis of twenty years of consulting. It integrates best practices from consulting firms, colleagues, and clients. I would first like to acknowledge Accenture and PricewaterhouseCoopers for providing practical opportunities for me to learn and build strong skills in consulting, organizational change, large-scale systems change, and strategic thinking, among many others. It was this solid foundation that allowed me to create this methodology.

As a theoretical foundation, I worked with or studied the work of many thought leaders in the fields of leadership development, developmental psychology, integral theory, and others. The theoretical giants on whose hard work we built the Innovative Leadership and Organizational Transformation models include: Terri O'Fallon, Ph.D., Susanne Cook-Greuter, Ph.D., Hilke Richmer, Ph.D., Roxanne Howe-Murphy, Ed.D., and Peter Senge, Ph.D., Cindy Wigglesworth Ph.D., and Ken Wilber. These leaders shared not only their theories, but ongoing guidance and encouragement helping to create a solid framework that is comprehensive and theoretically grounded.

Contributing authors who actually put pen to paper and helped to make this book a reality: Belinda Gore, Ph.D., Mark Palmer, Mike Sayre, MBA, B. Keith Speers, Ph.D., Jason Miller, and Mike Morrow-Fox, MBA.

Friends and colleagues who served as constant cheerleaders and editors, listened to stories and dreams about the book, and helped make it come to fruition. Steve Terrell Ed.D., Geoff Fitch, and Ralph Spitzen, MBA, offered particularly insightful feedback as subject matter experts.

The teachers, trainers, and mentors who taught how to lead—and when to follow.

Clients who participated as case studies, as well as Capital University MBA students who gave feedback on the book by virtue of doing graduate work using the *Fieldbook* and writing articles that are incorporated into the foundation for this book.

Family who inspired me to be thoughtful, dedicated to work, and to contribute to the world in a meaningful way.

Publisher and friend, Russ Volckmann, Ph.D.

Graphic design and layout firm Creative Spot, copy editor Sara Phelps, as well as editors, reviewers, endorsers, thought partners, and countless others who spent untold hours making this possible.

Table of Contents

FOREWORD

Innovative Leaders Guide to Transforming Organizations

Maureen Metcalf has done it again. The *Innovative Leaders Guide to Transforming Organizations* is a gift to leaders who are serious about transforming themselves while simultaneously transforming their organizations. As with Metcalf's earlier books, this guide is replete with tools, models, questions, processes, work plans, and reflections about the inner and outer work that's necessary to make systemic change that lasts.

Today, more than ever before, organizations are overwhelmed by the pace of change. Just keeping up with technology and fierce competition in the marketplace is exhausting. Everything "out there" seems daunting. But, brilliantly, Metcalf doesn't start "out there." She starts "in here" with an internal focus on the leader using the Enneagram. Rooted in fourth century Greece and refined in the 1950s, the Enneagram is a personality trait tool that can lead to better understanding of self and the dynamics at play in personal or business relationships. With this, Metcalf invites readers to explore who they are and what internal and inherent motivations are the basis for decisions, responses, and behaviors in interactions.

From this self-knowledge, leaders begin the exploration of change in Leadership Behaviors and development, and prepare for a hard organizational change.

The first half of the guide is devoted to exploring and discovering personality traits and types, Developmental Perspective, behaviors, and mindset. And, appropriately, there is a focus on Resilience—because it takes incredible resilience to lead an organization through transformative change. In fact, if truth be known, there's probably no leader who, in the middle of the change, hasn't wished that he had never started it. Transformative change is tough work with most of it playing out behind the scenes.

This guide is designed to organize the chaos that accompanies transformative and systemic change. Metcalf delineates the process into seven categories that are straightforward and easy to follow. She gives templates to help group the work. She offers examples and tells stories of how this method has worked. And, more importantly, she illustrates and integrates the personal "inside" work of the leader with the "outside" work of the organization. We're introduced to Paul, an executive who takes his organization through transformative change, and are privy to the conversation Paul has with himself as he applies what he has learned about himself and what he learns about his organization: What do I do? What do I believe? How do we do this?

As a change management professional, I can attest to the truth and efficacy of the *Innovative Leaders Guide to Transforming Organizations*. Whether you are an executive getting ready to lead the change, a consultant helping a company go through change, or a professional in an organization participating in the change, this guide provides you with a map that will sometimes take you off the beaten path to places you never imagined or may never have found on your own. The journey is just beginning—embrace it!

– Carla Paonessa

Chair, LeaderShape Board of Directors and
Retired Managing Partner, Accenture

INTRODUCTION
Using Innovative Leadership to Transform Your Organization

The Challenge

> *"Today any company that isn't rethinking its direction at least every few years—as well as constantly adjusting to changing contexts—and then quickly making significant operational changes is putting itself at risk. But, as any number of business leaders can attest, the tension between needing to stay ahead of increasingly fierce competition and needing to deliver this year's results can be overwhelming."*
>
> —*John P. Kotter, Konosuke Matsushita Professor of Leadership, Emeritus, Harvard Business School, Harvard Business Review (2012)*

Accelerating change continues to impact every facet of business. To thrive long term, business leaders must make implementing change a core competency enabling them to capitalize on our changing world instead of merely attempting to adapt to it.

In attempts to stay abreast of rapid changes, continuous advancements in systems' efficiencies have been enabled by unprecedented rates of technology development. The ensuing race to keep pace with competitors and technology has proven deeply problematic as innovating functional efficiencies has become the singular focus of corporate strategy at the expense of vision and cultural cohesion. Significant dissonance between day-to-day functioning and purpose has arisen as companies have focused their energies on performance training rather than the development of sophisticated thinking, complex interaction capabilities, or comprehensive decision-making skills. In essence, organizational strategy has been reduced to improving functional processes, and technical competency has inappropriately become equivalent to strategic vision.

This shallow version of strategy has not only driven market volatility, it has worked to marginalize new organizational strategies, particularly those emerging to address the flattening global economy. Companies are applying more technology innovation to resolve issues that were created by a myopic focus on innovating technology.

Companies clearly need innovation to successfully navigate the new economic landscape—and they are not getting it. It's relatively rare for transformation programs to deliver the results that were projected in the original business case.

> *"It's relatively rare for transformation programs to succeed; many surveys, including our own, put the success rate at less than 40 percent. Our recent research, however, underscores the fact that certain tactics promote successful outcomes. The most important tactics are setting clear and high aspirations and targets, exercising strong leadership from the top, creating an unambiguous structure for the transformation, and maintaining energy and involvement throughout the organization. Companies that used all of these tactics succeeded more than 80 percent of the time."*
>
> *—McKinsey Quarterly, April 2009*

Simply put, companies attempting to traverse the new economic landscape with incomplete tactics will not succeed. We integrate these findings and others into our recommendations throughout this book. In addition to looking at tactics used to implement change, we also need to look at the impact leadership has on the organization's ability to successfully implement change.

> *"After conducting fourteen formal studies and more than a thousand interviews, directly observing dozens of executives in action, and compiling innumerable surveys, I am completely convinced that most organizations today lack the leadership they need...And the shortfall is often large. I'm not talking about a deficit of 10%, but of 200%, 400%, or more in positions up and down the hierarchy." (Kotter)*

More comprehensive approaches to leadership and organizational transformation must be seriously considered. An exclusive focus on systems' performance and analytics can prove costly. Enhancing organizational capacity must extend beyond increasing system functionality.

> *"Change-management processes supplement the system we know. They can slide easily into a project-management organization. They can be made stronger or faster by adding more resources, more sophisticated versions of the same old methods, or smarter people to drive the process—but again—only up to a point. After that point, using this approach to launch strategic initiatives that ask an organization to absorb more change faster can create confusion, resistance, fatigue, and higher costs." (Kotter, 2012)*

If, in addition to developing better functional processes, _you also begin to clarify strategic vision, grow leadership capacity, and build a cohesive company culture—you will achieve much greater and more sustainable success._

Of course not every challenge requires a leader to change how he thinks about the business or themselves as a leader to "solve" it, but many complex challenges do. One of the biggest challenges for today's leader is developing the ability to identify which problems require complex solutions and which ones are merely technical in nature and can be solved using more traditional approaches. Developing complex solutions requires experimentation and often generates new discoveries. These solutions can take a long time to implement and are rarely successfully implemented by edict. To succeed in developing complex solutions, leaders need to fully understand the organization's problems and challenges and their own leadership capabilities along with understanding the barriers and resistance they will likely face.

Complex challenges illuminate deeply held beliefs and force not only a change in how work is done but also in the leaders themselves and an organization's values. What results is more than a process change or innovation translation. A complex solution will create changes in processes, but also in personal values and beliefs, behaviors, and interactions. Solutions to complex challenges that are most effective are those that change the leader and the organization's _relationship_ to processes, values, behaviors, and interactions. In other words, the change process works on the leader at the same time the leader works on the change.

> **"Leaders must be willing to face what they will need to change about themselves as well as change about their organizations to successfully solve adaptive challenges."**
>
> **—Ronald A. Heifetz and Donald A. Laurie, "The Work of Leadership"**
> **Harvard Business Review Breakthrough Leadership, December 2001**

As the term suggests, "adaptive challenges" require leaders and employees to learn new ways of thinking about the work as well as new ways of doing the work. Adaptive challenges are often the most elusive as they require that we change not only the organization but take on the difficult process of looking at ourselves as leaders and determine how we need to change in order to solve the challenge we are facing. We will use the terms "adaptive change" and "transformation" throughout this guide to mean complex changes that requires a solution involving change to the leader, the culture, and the organizational systems. Heifetz and Laurie built on these initial findings in their June 2009 book, *The Practice of Adaptive Leadership: Tools and Tactics for Changing Your Organization and the World.*

The Solution

This guide is based on a synthesis of several models and the principles they put forth into a process and series of questions a leader can ask to guide his actions when dealing with adaptive challenges.

Jim Collins, the bestselling business author of *Good to Great* and *Great by Choice*, says leadership is critical to effectively move organizations to greatness. He uses terms like Level 5 Leader and 10x Leader to refer to the type of leadership required to successfully implement adaptive change. In his books, Collins starts with leadership as the foundation for effective transformation.

According to Kotter in this November 2012 *Harvard Business Review* article, one of the five principles of accelerating change is:

> *"...much more leadership, not just more management. At the core of a successful hierarchy is competent management. A strategy network, by contrast, needs lots of leadership, which means it operates with different processes and language and expectations. The game is all about vision, opportunity, agility, inspired action, and celebration— not project management, budget reviews, reporting relationships, compensation, and accountability to a plan....The new operating system continually assesses the business, the industry, and the organization, and reacts with greater agility, speed, and creativity than the existing one. It complements rather than overburdens the traditional hierarchy, thus freeing the latter to do what it's optimized to do. It actually makes enterprises easier to run and accelerates strategic change. This is not an "either or" idea. It's "both and." I'm proposing two systems that operate in concert."*

Kotter's concept of a dual operating system moving beyond hierarchy to a networked model of operation is addressed in our Innovative Leadership Model.

Innovative Leadership and the Art of Leading Change

The concept of leading change starts with leadership and yet in many organizations the process of leading change often omits the idea that transforming leaders is part of the overall transformation process. This book starts with an approach to leadership that we call innovative leadership. It is a comprehensive model defining the five key elements required to successfully address adaptive challenges and transform organizations to solve these challenges.

Leadership Behaviors

Situational Analysis

Resilience

Developmental Perspective

Leader Type

Leveraging the focus of key researchers along with our change implementation experience, we focus on building innovative leadership as the foundation for implementing adaptive change. We define innovative leadership as the ability to influence by engaging equally across the four key dimensions: intention, behavior, culture, and systems. This ability is developed by addressing the five elements in the image to the left.

Innovative leadership is also based on the recognition that four dimensions (intention, behavior, culture, and systems) exist in all experiences, and already influence every interactive experience we have. To deny the interplay of any one of the four dimensions is missing the full picture. You can only build innovative leadership by simultaneously addressing all four dimensions.

Because innovative leadership influences by engaging the four dimensions equally, innovative leaders are uniquely qualified to implement adaptive change with a much higher success rate. A primary reason for transformation failure is that leaders focus primarily on the systems, rather than the larger context that includes themselves as leader and the organizational culture.

Section I of the guide is focused on individual leadership to help you build an understanding of what innovative leadership is and how you can apply it to solve adaptive problems. We explore each of the five elements in detail and give examples of how you, as an innovative leader, can use these elements in your transformation effort.

Section II of the guide focuses on the process of leading transformative change to address adaptive challenges. This section puts innovative leadership to work by building on what we learned in Section I. It provides a change model and gives an example of how an innovative leader implements transformative change. It is designed to offer a change model and practical tools and steps that you can use to lead change.

This model (shown below) is based on a combination of approaches including Kotter's model in *Leading Change*, Heifitz and Laurie's model from their paper "The Work of Leadership," and Ken Wilber's integral model. While our model appears to be linear in nature, the timing may not be, as steps may happen concurrently—and in some cases are repeated for multiple audiences—and one step may not be complete when another is started.

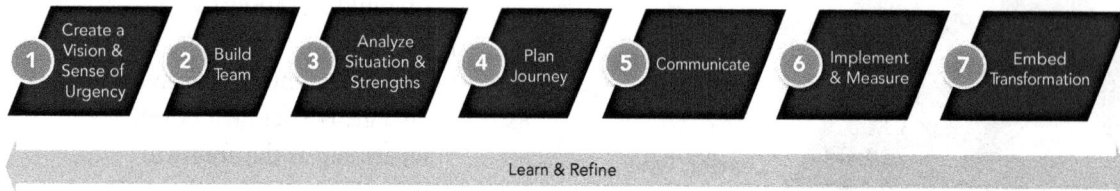

1 Create a Vision & Sense of Urgency 2 Build Team 3 Analyze Situation & Strengths 4 Plan Journey 5 Communicate 6 Implement & Measure 7 Embed Transformation

Learn & Refine

Implementing substantial transformative change is the work of innovative leaders, leading a skilled team of people, to accomplish a goal that will become more finely tuned during the implementation process. To add to the complexity, these projects are more successful when implemented outside of the corporate hierarchy using networks of people and projects that are interdependent on one another. The purpose of this book is to give you—as an innovative leader—a high-level understanding of the change process and how to lead change; it is not intended to teach you the nuts and bolts of how to manage the project or the change effort as part of the project team.

Benefits

By combining innovative leadership with a comprehensive change model where the leader equally considers the four dimensions, implementing transformative change to solve adaptive problems will have a higher success rate. This higher success rate is possible because this new model accomplishes the following:

- Addresses adaptive problems by analyzing them and developing comprehensive solutions beyond those found in traditional problem-solving approaches;

- Addresses the four dimensions: a leader's intention and behavior along with the organization's culture and systems in a systematic manner that creates alignment between them;

- Includes the innovative leader in the change process: expecting the leader to innovate how they lead to keep pace with the challenges they are solving.

During this era of increased complexity, an accelerated need for change, and failed change initiatives, it is critical for organizations to identify new models which address these challenges while concurrently maintaining efficient and effective operations and have a higher likelihood of yielding successful and sustained change.

REFLECTION QUESTIONS

What adaptive challenges does your organization face?

How does your organization integrate leadership development into the transformation process?

What is your leadership role in implementing change?

Do you have any experience in aligning an organization across the four domains, your intention and action, the organization's culture and systems?

Defining an Innovative Leader

Because innovative leadership is a critical foundation to this model, we want to start with the definition. What are specific qualities that differentiate an innovative leader from a traditional leader? In this era of rapid business, social, and ecological change, a successful innovative leader is a leader who can consistently:

- Clarify and effectively articulate vision
- Link that vision to attainable strategic initiatives
- Develop himself and influence the development of other leaders
- Build effective teams by helping colleagues realize and act on their own leadership strengths
- Cultivate alliances and partnerships
- Anticipate and aggressively respond both to challenges and opportunities
- Develop robust and resilient solutions
- Develop and test hypotheses
- Measure, learn, and refine on an ongoing basis

To further illustrate some of the qualities of innovative leadership, we offer this comparison between traditional leadership and innovative leadership:

TRADITIONAL LEADERSHIP	INNOVATIVE LEADERSHIP
Leader is guided primarily by desire for personal success and peripherally by organizational success	Leader is humbly guided by a more altruistic vision of success based on both performance and the value of the company's positive impact
Leadership decision style is command and control—leader has all the answers	Leader leverages team for answers as an adjunct to decision-making process, motivating people to perform through strategic focus, mentoring and coaching, and interpersonal intelligence
Leader chooses a course in "black/white" manner; tends to dogmatically stay the course	Leader perceives and behaves like a scientist continually measuring and testing for improvement
Leader focuses on being technically correct and in charge	Leader is continually learning and developing self and others
Leader tends to the numbers and quantitative measures that drive those numbers	Leader tends to financial performance, customer satisfaction, employee engagement, community impact, and cultural cohesion

Getting the Most from this Guide

Before you get started, take a moment to think about why you purchased this guide. Setting goals and understanding your intentions and expectations about the exercises will help you focus on identifying and driving your desired results.

In order to help clarify, consider the following questions:

- What are the five to seven events and/or choices that brought you to where you are professionally and personally?
- How did these events or choices contribute to choosing to buy and use this guide?
- What stands out in the list you have made? Are there any surprises or patterns?
- What do you hope to gain from your investment in the transformation process?

- What is your greatest growth need with regard to leading transformative change?
- What is your greatest fear if the transformation does not deliver the impact you anticipate?
- What meaningful impact will success or failure produce in your professional career and personal life?

In addition to reflecting on the above questions, here are some ideas we recommend to help you get the most out of this experience. It is our experience that people who adhere to the following agreements tend to have a deeper and more enriching overall experience. By participating in this fashion, you will generate a richer evaluation of yourself and most effectively take advantage of what this fieldbook has to offer.

Take a moment to reflect on the guidelines below:

AGREEMENT	RELATED ACTION OR BEHAVIOR
1. Be fully present	Let go of thoughts about other activities while you read. Bring your full attention to the work
2. Take responsibility for your own success	Be 100% responsible for the outcome of your engagement with this material
3. Participate as fully as possible	Complete all the exercises to the best of your abilities. Apply the concepts and skills that work best for you, and modify those that do not
4. Practice good life management	Invest time at scheduled intervals to work on the materials when you are mentally and emotionally at your best
5. Lean into optimal discomfort; take risks without overwhelming yourself.	Be candid, open, and direct. Allow yourself to be curious and vulnerable
6. Take the process seriously, and more importantly take yourself lightly. Make this positive and rewarding experience.	Allow yourself balance. Find the lesson and humor in both your successes and mistakes. Most importantly, have fun!

How to Use this Guide

After this introduction, each subsequent chapter builds to form a complete approach to implementing transformative change. The first section of the book provides the conceptual framework. The second section guides you through a series of exercises to help ground those ideas in a more practical fashion. We recommend that you use the following sequence to help efficiently process the material:

1. Read Intently

Read through the chapter completely as we introduce and illustrate an integrated set of concepts for each element in building innovative leadership.

2. Contemplate

Using a set of carefully chosen applications and specifically designed exercises will help you to embody the work and bring the concepts to life. Through a process of dynamic examination and reflection, you will be encouraged to contemplate some significant, real-life implications of change. Many of the exercises can be done on your own while others are designed to be conducted with input from your colleagues.

3. Link Together Your Experience

As you sequentially build your understanding, you will begin noticing habits and conditioned patterns that can present you with clear opportunities for growth. Though you may encounter personal resistance along the way, you will also discover new and exciting strengths. Once you have completed the process, you will have created a plan to transform your organization (or a portion of the organization). Ultimately, implementing that plan will be up to you and your team.

As you become more adept at using these ideas, you will find yourself increasingly capable of engaging with the concepts proactively along with an ability and greater capacity to respond to situations requiring innovative leadership to implement a series of changes.

4. Worksheets

Throughout this guide, the pencil icon indicates worksheets for your individual use. Copies of these worksheets with additional space for your answers are in the Appendix.

Leadership Behaviors

Situational Analysis

Resilience

Developmental Perspective

Leader Type

SECTION I

Five Elements of Innovative Leadership

This section comprises the first five chapters of this guide and is the section in which we explore the five elements of innovative leadership in greater depth. These elements (chapters) are reflected in the graphic above. You will be using them as an individual leader, in your work with the leadership team, and also in the organization as you implement transformative change.

Each chapter offers a definition of the key element, explains the role it plays in using innovative leadership to transform organizations, gives an example of the models we use, and provides a case study to demonstrate how we have applied these elements to improve leadership and transform organizations. These five key elements are interconnected and must be considered as a whole to build truly innovative leadership.

This model also serves as the foundation for Section II in which you will put your innovative leadership skills to work as you transform your organization.

Innovative Leadership Assessment

Leadership Behaviors
Situational Analysis
Resilience
Developmental Perspective
Leader Type

Following is a short self assessment to help you identify your own innovative leadership scores. It is organized by the five domains of innovative leadership and will give you a general sense of where you need to focus your efforts to improve your innovative leadership capacity. As you progress through the book, there is information on the full assessments if you are interested in a more in-depth and thorough analysis of your current capacity.

We encourage you to take this assessment as a way to get a snapshot of where you excel and where you may want to focus your developmental activities and energies.

Score Yourself on Awareness of Leader Type and Self-Management

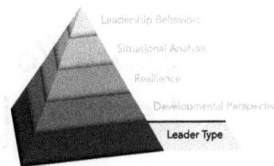

Think about your level of response to work situations over the past year and answer the following questions using this scale:

Never (1)   *Rarely (2)*   *Sometimes (3)*   *Often (4)*   *Almost always (5)*

1. I have taken a leadership type assessment such as the Enneagram, Myers-Briggs Type Indicator or DISC, and used this information about myself to increase my effectiveness.

   1 2 3 4 5

2. I use the insight from this assessment to understand my type—specifically, I understand my gifts and limitations, and try to leverage my strengths and manage my limitations.

   1 2 3 4 5

3. I have a reflection practice where I understand, actively monitor and work with my "fixations" (a fixation is a negative thought pattern).

   1 2 3 4 5

4. I have a clear sense of who I am and what I want to contribute in the world.

   1 2 3 4 5

5. I manage my emotional reactions to allow me to respond with socially appropriate behavior.

   1 2 3 4 5

6. I am aware of what causes me stress and actively manage it.

   1 2 3 4 5

7. I have positive coping strategies.

   1 2 3 4 5

8. I actively seek ways to feel empowered even when the organization may not.

   1 2 3 4 5

Total Score

- If your overall score in this category is 24 or less, it's time to pay attention to your leadership type and self management.

- If your overall score in this category is 25–31, you are in the healthy range, but could still benefit from some focus on your leadership type and self-management.

- If your overall score is 32 or above, Congratulations! You are self-aware and using your leadership type to increase your effectiveness.

Score Yourself on Developmental Perspective Aligned with Innovation

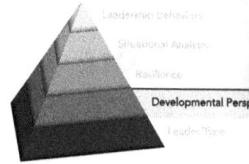

Think about your level of response to work situations over the past year and answer the following questions using this scale:

Never (1)   Rarely (2)   Sometimes (3)   Often (4)   Almost always (5)

1. I have a sense of life purpose and do work that is generally aligned with that purpose.   1 2 3 4 5

2. I am motivated more by the impact I make on the world rather than on personal notoriety.   1 2 3 4 5

3. I try to live my life according to my personal values.   1 2 3 4 5

4. I believe that collaboration across groups and organizations is important to accomplish our goals.   1 2 3 4 5

5. I believe that getting business results must be balanced with treating people fairly and kindly, as well as making a positive impact on our customers and community.   1 2 3 4 5

6. I seek input from others consistently to test my thinking and expand my perspective.   1 2 3 4 5

7. I think about the impact of my work on the many elements of our community and beyond.   1 2 3 4 5

8. I am open and curious, always trying new things and learning from all of them.   1 2 3 4 5

9. I appreciate the value of rules and am willing to question them in a professional manner.   1 2 3 4 5

Total Score

- ◢ If your overall score in this category is 27 or less, it's time to pay attention to your developmental level including testing your current level and focusing on developing in the area of developmental perspectives.

- ◢ If your overall score in this category is 28–35, you are in the healthy range, but could still benefit from some focus on developing in the area of developmental perspectives.

- ◢ If your score is 36 or above, Congratulations! Your developmental level appears to be aligned with innovative leadership, yet this assessment is only a subset of a full assessment.

Score Yourself on Resilience

Think about your level of response to work situations over the past year and answer the following questions using this scale:

Never (1)   Rarely (2)   Sometimes (3)   Often (4)   Almost always (5)

1. I consistently take care of my physical needs such as getting enough sleep and exercise.
   1 2 3 4 5

2. I have a sense of purpose and get to do activities that contribute to that purpose daily.
   1 2 3 4 5

3. I have a high degree of self-awareness and manage my thoughts actively.
   1 2 3 4 5

4. I have a strong support system consisting of a healthy mix of friends, colleagues, and family.
   1 2 3 4 5

5. I can reframe challenges to find something of value in most situations.
   1 2 3 4 5

6. I build strong trusting relationships at work.
   1 2 3 4 5

7. I am aware of my own self-talk and actively manage it.
   1 2 3 4 5

8. I have a professional development plan that includes gaining skills and acquiring additional perspectives.
   1 2 3 4 5

Total Score

- If your overall score in this category is 24 or less, it's time to pay attention to your resilience.

- If your overall score in this category is 25–31, you are in the healthy range, but could still benefit from some focus on resilience.

- If your score is 32 or above, Congratulations! You are likely performing well in the area of Resilience, yet this assessment is only a subset of the full resilience assessment.

Score Yourself on Situational Analysis

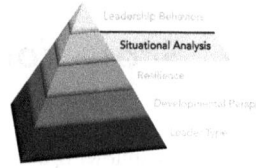

Think about your level of response to work situations over the past year and answer the following questions using this scale:

Never (1)   Rarely (2)   Sometimes (3)   Often (4)   Almost always (5)

1. I am aware of my own passions and values.

2. My behavior consistently reflects my goals and values.

   1 2 3 4 5

3. I feel safe pushing back when I am asked to do things that are not aligned with my values.

   1 2 3 4 5

4. I am aware that my behavior and decisions as a leader have an impact on the people I work with (even if I am not directly managing people).

   1 2 3 4 5

5. I am deliberate about aligning my behaviors with the behaviors (and results) the organization values and I pay attention to delivering the desired results.

   1 2 3 4 5

6. I am aware of how my values align with those of the organization and where they are misaligned; if there are misalignments, I try to find constructive ways address these differences.

   1 2 3 4 5

Total Score

◢ If your overall score in this category is 18 or less, it's time to pay attention to your alignment with the organization and also the alignment of culture and systems within the organization that you are able to impact.

◢ If your overall score in this category is 19–23, you are in the healthy range, but could still benefit from some focus on alignment.

◢ If your score is 24 or above, Congratulations! You are well-aligned with the organization and the organization's culture and systems are well-aligned.

Score Yourself on Leadership Behaviors

Think about your level of response to work situations over the past year and answer the following questions using this scale:

Never (1)   *Rarely (2)*   *Sometimes (3)*   *Often (4)*   *Almost always (5)*

1. I tend to be proactive—I anticipate what is coming next and actively manage it. (This may be primarily in my personal life.)   1 2 3 4 5

2. I focus on creating results in a way that helps me grow and develop along with those who work for me while accomplishing our tasks.   1 2 3 4 5

3. I think about the impact of my actions on the organization rather than just getting the job done.   1 2 3 4 5

4. I see how my work contributes to organizational success.   1 2 3 4 5

5. I deliberately try to improve myself and the organization.   1 2 3 4 5

6. I take time to mentor others, veven when I am busy (this could be formal or informal mentoring).   1 2 3 4 5

7. I consider myself a personal learner because of the time I spend reading and trying new ideas and activities. I am curious.   1 2 3 4 5

8. I have the courage to speak out in a professional manner when asked to do something with which I disagree.   1 2 3 4 5

9. I accomplish results by working with and through others in a positive and constructive manner.   1 2 3 4 5

Total Score

◗ If your overall score in this category is 27 or less, it's time to pay attention to your leadership behaviors and look for ways to develop in alignment with your goals.

◗ If your overall score in this category is 28–35, you are in the healthy range, but could still benefit from some focus on your leadership behaviors.

◗ If your score is 36 or above, Congratulations! You are likely performing well in the area of leadership behaviors, but this assessment is only a subset of a full leadership behavior assessment.

CHAPTER 1

Leader Type

Fig. 1.1 Five Elements of Innovative Leadership

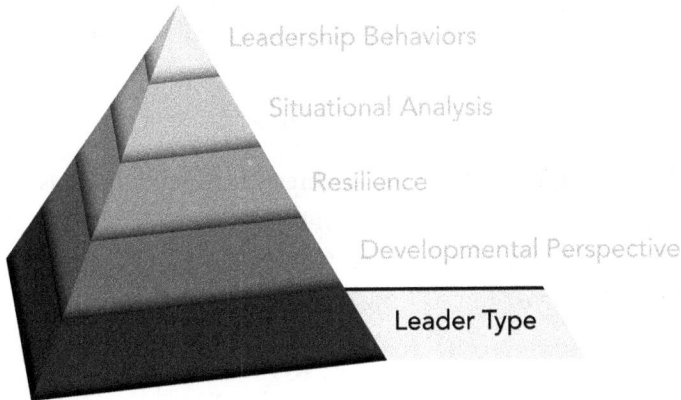

Leadership Behaviors

Situational Analysis

Resilience

Developmental Perspective

Leader Type

Sarah was the vice president of marketing for a Fortune 100 company when we met several years ago. She was easily recognizable throughout her division for the bright colors that she wore and for her equally bright disposition, and her skill at making people feel instantly comfortable was acknowledged and appreciated. Sarah rose through the ranks in the company starting out as a sales assistant, and then earning progressively more responsibility. As an executive, she was centered, focused, and highly successful. Her office was an interesting fusion of beautifully crafted cherry furniture, professional certifications and awards, and personal memorabilia honoring both work and family relationships. The office was neatly organized despite the obvious well use that it received.

Sarah's warm green eyes shined through the lenses of her stylish black glasses as she started the conversation. After first courteously asking about my work and my family, her demeanor became serious. "I wanted to meet with you today because I am very concerned about one of my senior directors," she began. "He was a top salesman when he came to us and was quickly moved into our high-achievers program. His numbers were always solid and his group was very productive when he was a manager." At that, she looked down reflectively and then back to me. "But even then," she remarked, "I would hear about incidents where people left meetings feeling demoralized. He has such strong people skills and is so bright; I thought that these incidents must have been attempts to help his staff stretch. Now, in retrospect, I think I missed some warning signs. We are at the point where he has stepped on so many toes that nobody wants to work with him."

At this point Sarah's posture shifted and she leaned into the conversation. "Even worse," she said emphatically, "he seems totally unaware that his behaviors and decision-making style put people off. After talking with him and several members of his team, I've realized that he feels that his charm and intelligence are all that he needs. He really has no idea that he is burning important bridges. Right now, he continues to put his career at risk and will certainly make his—in fact, our—long-term success unattainable." She sat silently for a moment as she collected her final thoughts, then asked, "Is there any way that you can help him become self aware enough to resurrect his reputation?"

Of course there was. Yet, problems like those of this senior director are as complex as they are common. He had all of the technical skills, intelligence, and the motivation to be a very effective leader. However, staff turnover, poor collaboration, and a reputation of being difficult to work with find him doing as much harm to his company as good.

The Importance of Leader Type

Part of the challenge in building innovative leadership is learning to leverage the clarity of your introspection. Looking inside yourself and examining the makeup of your inner being, enables you to function in a highly-grounded way, rather than operating from the innate biases of uninformed decision-making.

First and foremost start by simply considering your disposition, tendencies, inclinations, and ways of being. Innovative leadership hinges on understanding the simple, native manner in which you show up in your life. One way to observe this is by examining key aspects of your inner being, often called Leader Type, which reflect a leader's personality type. The Leader Personality Type (going forward referred to as Leader Type) critically influences who you are as a leader. It is an essential foundation of your personal makeup and greatly shapes the effectiveness of your leadership. The ancient adage "Know thyself" holds true as a crucial underpinning in leadership performance.

When the sixty-five member Advisory Council for the Stanford Graduate School of Business was polled several years ago on the topic of what is most important to include in the school's curriculum—weighing all the tools of the MBA trade including forecasting, strategic planning, and financial analysis, among many, many others—there was an overwhelming, and quite impressive, agreement that the most important thing business school graduates needed to learn was self-awareness and the resulting ability to reduce denial in their perceptions of themselves and their actions. This speaks to the emerging deep recognition that we are highlighting in Innovative Leadership: Leaders, through their own personality quirks and biases, can derail the most progressive initiatives toward an organization's sustainable success.

Your ability to use deep introspection relies on your development of and a capacity for self-understanding and self-awareness. Both allow you profound openness of personal perspective as well as a greater understanding of others. These critical traits support leaders' abilities to self-regulate, communicate effectively with others, and encourage personal learning. Employing a deeper understanding of Leader Type for both yourself and others is a powerful tool to promote effective leadership.

It is important to keep in mind that this particular notion of type is inherent to your being and generally does not change significantly over the course of your life. This is an essential point: by ascertaining the distinct "shape" of your type, as well as that of others around you, you can begin to see situations without the bias of your own perceptions. You are then in a better position to leverage what you and others actually demonstrate, rather than acting from speculation. You learn to deeply understand the inner shifts in your strengths, weaknesses, and core patterns. Typing tools are helpful in promoting this kind of self-knowledge and pattern recognition.

> *By learning about these patterns, you can gain perspective on your life and start connecting the dots among your different experiences. Most of us have a concept about how we behave, but that idea is likely clouded and not entirely true. One of the hardest things for most people is to see themselves accurately. How astonishing it is to see through the clouds and recognize yourself clearly.*
>
> *—Roxanne Howe Murphy, Deep Living (2013)*

Learning at this deeper level, as patterns appear within your immediate experience, can offer remarkable insights about areas of life that, in your personal experience, you may tend to exaggerate or overemphasize.

Self-awareness and the capacity for self-management are foundational to innovative leadership and overall leadership effectiveness. By becoming aware of your inherent gifts as well as those of others, you are able to improve your personal effectiveness and the personal effectiveness of the teams and departments with which you work.

The Enneagram

Fig. 1.2

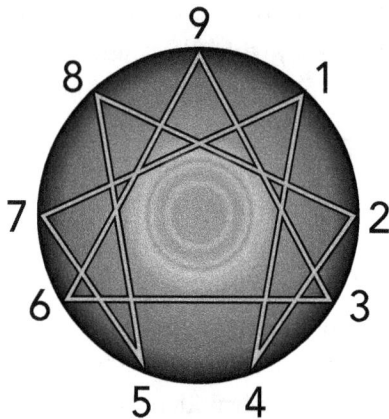

Our preferred model for exploring self-awareness in leaders is the Enneagram system of personality types. The name "Enneagram" derives from the Greek for nine (ennea) and for a figure (grama); hence, the Enneagram symbol is a circle with nine equidistant points around the circumference connected by internal lines that create an equilateral triangle, joining points. Using the symbol as a map, we can describe patterns of personality as well as highly effective pathways for personal change.

According to Belinda Gore, "In my experience using the Enneagram system as a psychologist and a leadership coach over the past twenty-three years, I find it to be more robust than any other system I have encountered." Many organizations are familiar with DISC, MBTI, Social Styles, and other systems, and training in these models has given employees at every level of an organization a foundation in psychological models for self-awareness and an appreciation for the diversity within teams. Gore found leaders at every level able to readily learn the rich and versatile information the Enneagram offers.

The Enneagram, like other tools, offers a framework and language to discuss what you perceive about intentions and what you see in your own and others' behaviors. Each Enneagram type is based on a pattern of what you pay attention to, or more specifically, your naturally occurring perceptions and preferences. By understanding the types of experiences you habitually reinforce and put energy into, you can observe yourself more accurately and develop greater self-awareness. ***By enhancing self-awareness, you can make choices about your own actions rather than engaging in patterns of automatic thought, emotion, and behavior out of habitual and unconscious responses.*** This insight alone will allow you to tailor personal and professional goals to achieve better results.

We recommend you take an Enneagram assessment to determine your type. You can find a simplified free version and a full-length test at www.enneagraminstitute.com. You will likely have high scores in two to three areas, in some cases more. Please read the links provided by the Enneagram Institute as well as the balance of this chapter to narrow down your type. You may also want to ask your colleagues to take the assessment to determine how your strengths and theirs complement one another.

The following table provides a brief description of the nine types and will serve as the basis for discussion in the balance of the chapter. We have provided a quick reference sheet at the end of this chapter where you can mark your scores; you may also want to detach the page and refer to it as you read the chapter.

In this chapter, we group the nine types using several different categorizations to demonstrate how this tool can be used to help you become a more self-aware leader and build your team effectiveness. For many leaders, these tools are best learned through application so we encourage you to find a small group interested in using the material.

Table 1.1

ENNEAGRAM TYPES

Type 1 — Reformer: The Rational, Idealistic Type

II am a principled, idealistic type. I am conscientious and ethical with a strong sense of right and wrong behavior. I can be a teacher, crusader, and advocate for change always striving to improve things, but sometimes afraid of making mistakes. Well-organized, orderly and fastidious, I try to maintain high standards, but can slip into being critical and perfectionistic. I typically have problems with resentment and impatience.

At My Best: I am wise, discerning, realistic, and noble. I can be morally heroic.

Type 2 — Helper: The Caring, Interpersonal Type

I am a caring, interpersonal type. I am empathetic, sincere, and warm-hearted. I am friendly, generous, and self-sacrificing, but can also be sentimental, flattering, and people-pleasing. I am well-meaning and driven to be close to others, but can slip into doing things for others in order to be needed. I typically have problems with possessiveness and with acknowledging my own needs.

At My Best: I am unselfish and altruistic, and have unconditional love for others.

Type 3 — Achiever: The Success-Oriented, Pragmatic Type

I am an adaptable, success-oriented type. I am self-assured, attractive, and charming. Ambitious, competent, and energetic, I can also be status-conscious and highly driven for advancement. I am diplomatic and poised, but can also be overly concerned with my image and what others think of me. I typically have problems with over focus on work and competitiveness.

At My Best: I am self-accepting, authentic, and a role model who inspires others.

Type 4 — Individualist: The Sensitive, Withdrawn Type

II am an introspective, romantic type. I am self-aware, sensitive, and reserved. I am emotionally honest, creative, and personal, but can also be moody and self-conscious. Withholding myself from others due to feeling vulnerable, I can also feel scornful and exempt from ordinary ways of living. I typically have problems with melancholy, self-indulgence, and self-pity.

At My Best: I am inspired and highly creative, and am able to renew myself and transform my experiences.

Type 5 — Investigator: The Intense, Cerebral Type

I am a perceptive, cerebral type. I am alert, insightful, and curious. I am able to concentrate and focus on developing complex ideas and skills. Independent, innovative, and inventive, I can also become preoccupied with my thoughts and imaginary constructs. I can be detached, yet high-strung and intense. I typically have problems with eccentricity, nihilism, and isolation.

At My Best: I am a visionary pioneer, often ahead of my time, and able to see the world in an entirely new way.

Type 6 — Loyalist: The Committed, Security-Oriented Type

I am reliable, hardworking, responsible, security-oriented, and trustworthy. I am an excellent troubleshooter and can foresee problems and foster cooperation, but can also become defensive, evasive, and anxious running on stress while complaining about it. I can be cautious and indecisive, but also reactive, defiant, and rebellious. I typically have problems with self-doubt and suspicion.

At My Best: I am internally stable and self-reliant, courageously championing myself and others.

Type Seven — Enthusiast: The Busy, Fun-Loving Type

I am a busy, outgoing, productive type. I am extroverted, optimistic, versatile, and spontaneous. Playful, high-spirited, and practical, I can also misapply many talents, becoming over-extended, scattered, and undisciplined. I constantly seek new and exciting experiences, but can become distracted and exhausted by staying on the go. I typically have problems with impatience and impulsiveness.

At My Best: I focus my talents on worthwhile goals, becoming appreciative, joyous, and satisfied.

Type Eight — Challenger: The Powerful, Dominating Type

I am powerful, aggressive, self-confident, strong, and assertive. Protective, resourceful, straight talking, and decisive, I can also be egocentric and domineering. I feel I must control my environment, especially people, sometimes becoming confrontational and intimidating. I typically have problems with my temper and with allowing myself to be vulnerable.

At My Best: I am self-mastering and I use my strength to improve others' lives, becoming heroic, magnanimous, and inspiring.

Type Nine — Peacemaker: The Easygoing, Self-effacing Type

I am accepting, trusting, easy going, and stable. I am usually grounded, supportive and often creative, but can also be too willing to go along with others to keep the peace. I want everything to go smoothly and be without conflict, but can also tend to be complacent and emotionally distant, simplifying problems and ignoring anything upsetting. I typically have problems with inertia and stubbornness.

At My Best: I am indomitable and all-embracing and able to bring people together to heal conflicts.

It is likely that you have already recognized that each of us comprise ALL nine types in that we have all had experiences manifesting varying degrees of these patterns of behavior. The key to identifying a person's core Enneagram type is to look beyond behavior to the factors motivating that behavior. Through awareness of motivation we can predict the ways in which leaders and organizations sabotage their best efforts, as well as find the line of least resistance toward getting back on track.

Self-awareness, the practice of engaging in self-reflection and achieving clarity of insight, being conscious of one's own identity, and the extent to which perceptions about oneself are accurate and compatible with others' observations, play a pivotal role in leadership. Self-aware leaders self-regulate cognitions, emotions, and behavior more effectively depending on the situation, evaluate their impact on others, and possess higher levels of emotional intelligence.

Thus, they become more versatile in their leadership and may perform better. Consequently, successful leader development is foremost personal development. The Enneagram, one of the most comprehensive systems for understanding personality [Leader Type] and human development, offers considerable merit to support leaders to become more aware of themselves and others.

—Hilke Richmer, Ed.D. (2012)

As we observed through Richmer's research project, the Enneagram can be a very powerful typing model. Let's continue to explore the concept of type by using the Enneagram as our primary tool.

One advantage of the Enneagram is that it is wonderfully organic—based in our bodies as well as brains. The nine personality styles are formed through a characteristic imbalance in the uses of the three primary centers of intelligence in the human body. While we typically think of the brain as the center of intelligence, advances in neuroanatomy have demonstrated that there is also a complex of nerves in the solar plexus region that forms another center of body intelligence and a third complex of nerves in the center of the chest, known as the heart center of intelligence. These three centers align with the three major parts of the brain: the belly center aligns with the reptilian brain stem, responsible for instinctual behavior and home of the autonomic nervous system that controls arousal and relaxation; the heart center aligns with the mid-brain where the mechanism for fundamental emotion, as well as mirror neurons and limbic resonance account for our capacity for empathy; and, the head center aligns with the cerebral cortex, which includes the analytical and logical left lobe, as well as the holistic and intuitive right lobe. (These descriptions are of course very simplistic and we have listed resources in the bibliography for further exploration.)

In the Enneagram there are three triads, each linked with one of the centers of intelligence. Within each triad there are three personality types, each with a characteristic pattern of imbalance. We will explore these triads and their use in the application example provided later in the chapter.

Table 1.2

Triad	Default Position	Subdues Instinct	Focuses Triad
<u>Belly Center</u> manifests a desire for autonomy that translates as a focus on establishing and maintaining a boundary while using powerful, grounded, instinctual energy	Eight uses this center as a default position, overusing instinctual energy to dominate or overcome obstacles in the environment	Nine subdues instinctual energy in ourselves and others in order to mediate conflicts and maintain peace	One disciplines powerful instinctual drives toward serving ideals and principle
<u>Heart Center</u> specializes in establishing identity through emotion and interpersonal relationships	Two uses the heart center functions as the default position, tending to put overemphasis on establishing and maintaining connections with other people and relating to others in a nurturing emotional way	Three subdues personal emotions and longings to accomplish the goals that constitute others' ideas of success	Four focuses emotions toward the achievement of a sense of significance and identity
<u>Head Center</u> this center core characteristic is cognitive and serves to collect data for the purpose of predicting and managing the future	Five uses the head center as a default position, amassing data to support the role of expert and stepping back from the mundane in order to achieve distance and new insight	Six is inclined to subdue their own creative thinking as loyal and hardworking members of a larger group, using their mental capacities to identify possible problems in existing systems and work out solutions so the systems are not at risk	Type Seven focuses the head center energies on exploring options to optimize experiences

The Enneagram and Team Effectiveness

Organizations have "personality" types too. This is just another way to think about the organizational culture: the mission or role the organization seeks to fulfill, the favored strategies for accomplishing goals, the behaviors that are rewarded and those that are not, and the subtle hiring filters that tend to screen out people who do not fit. The senior leaders of the organization may or may not reflect the culture. It is immensely valuable for leaders to determine their organization's personality type to be able to harness the natural strengths of that pattern and avoid the imbedded tendencies that create problems. Leaders are likely to have a strong influence on the development of organizational culture, but without clear awareness they may not realize how the leader and the group are aligned and how they sometimes work in opposition.

Research using the Enneagram for Leadership Development and Organizational Effectiveness

Richmer used the Enneagram, a typing model, as the foundation to create a leadership development program and wrote about the results for her doctoral dissertation. According to Richmer:

> The purpose of the research was to assess the effects of the Personal Awareness and Effective Leadership Program in a medium-sized utility company in the Midwest United States. To provide middle managers with a unique development opportunity to enhance their awareness of self and others, the company had customized the Personal Awareness and Effective Leadership Program based on the Enneagram in 2009. The program was implemented in 2010.
>
> The company's organization development team conceived a program that focused on strengthening middle managers' interpersonal effectiveness and leadership versatility. Considering the extensive practical leadership experience of most middle managers and the challenge of actually changing leadership behavior, the team decided on a novel approach. Team members identified the Enneagram, one of the most comprehensive models of personality [Leader Type] and human development, as an appropriate instrument for the developmental program.

The Enneagram represented an accepted system to support middle managers to develop a better understanding of themselves and others. Therefore, teaching the Enneagram in leader development should foster middle managers' self-awareness and ultimately advance leadership behavior. This research evaluated the effects of the 2010 Personal Awareness and Effective Leadership Program for middle managers on enhancing self-awareness.

As a result of participating in the Personal Awareness and Effective Leadership Program, the company expected leaders to (a) understand the Enneagram and the nine [leader] personality types as identified by the Enneagram, be able to identify their own type, and realize their developmental path, (b) apply Enneagram and Situational Leadership knowledge in their leadership to better recognize motivations and values in themselves and others, and (c) become better equipped to consciously self-regulate behavior in leadership situations and communicate more effectively.

Her research concluded the following:

Participants in both cohorts [training groups] found the Enneagram valuable to understand the rationale for their own behavior as well as others' actions and reactions. Participants acknowledged that the Enneagram fostered the understanding of why we behave as we do and also how to best read others. One participant stated that to be an effective leader in today's workforce, you must be able to understand why you are the way you are, so that you can improve.

Richmer's experiment illustrates a crucial step toward building innovative leadership. To begin increasing your capacity for clear decision-making, you must first learn to impartially evaluate and examine the intentional and behavioral patterns in yourself as well as others. The inherent leverage within this simple yet powerful understanding cannot be overstated. It elicits a clarity that will help you make decisions without being governed by the bias of your own perceptions, even as you naturally experience them in any given occasion.

This objectivity is rooted in your ability to see your conditioning without preference. It is this nonjudgmental perspective that allows the nuances of experience to persist in the interest of gaining real understanding. When you begin seeing in this way, you can navigate skillfully and execute without the baggage of erroneous or false expectations.

It is important to note that while assessments can be very powerful tools, in some cases they may be used ineffectively. Before using assessments, it is critical that you understand how and when to use them. Whatever typing tool is employed, it should always be used to support and enhance awareness and appreciation of yourself and others. We have seen highly effective leaders of all personality types, so it is important to note that we are not recommending this tool to screen type for hiring or job placement within leadership roles and, obviously, it is unethical to use assessments to pigeon-hole, label, discriminate, or disadvantage people. Typing assessments are offered to benefit the individual and the team with personal growth and enhanced team effectiveness. We recommend that you share your Enneagram type with team members and colleagues to improve team and group dynamics. In addition to its effectiveness to improve self-awareness, it can also improve social interactions.

Applying a typing model can be an exceptionally valuable asset to team building and optimization. One of the critical challenges in working with teams is overcoming the conflicts of interest based on mischaracterization of team members. Such misconstrued perceptions can drain teams of precious energy as time is spent resolving conflict rather than attending to workloads and goals.

Application

Let's examine a very practical application within an organizational setting. A mid-sized utility company instituted leadership development training based on the Enneagram. The information provided in this section was used in the leadership development training to help leaders better understand themselves and their colleagues in order to perform more effectively.

In assessing several hundred people within the company, it became clear that the organization had a Type Six culture. The Type Six pattern is reflected in the company's mission to provide reliable and affordable gas and electric energy to their customers and to promote safety for their employees in power plants and in distribution. Loyalty, a trait of Type Six, is highly valued and many employees have worked for the company for twenty years or more. Attention is paid to identifying potential problems and working out solutions before they occur; when there is a power outage due to weather conditions, there is an expectation that the entire workforce will be available to provide support until the situation is resolved.

In some Enneagram training groups of individual contributors, up to fifty percent of the employees score themselves using an assessment tool along with classroom training and guided group discussion to have a Type Six personality (see Table 1.1 for summary of types). Among mid-level managers, that percentage drops to around thirty-five percent, and in the top group of senior leaders less than ten percent assess themselves as having the six personality pattern.

This is not unusual. Why? Because leaders in the C-suites (CEO, COO, CIO, CFO)—those who have risen to the top leadership levels—are not equally distributed around the Enneagram circle, but tend to cluster in another sub-grouping. The triads discussed earlier account for the underlying structure of each of the types related to the three centers of intelligence and how they function together, with one center taking a leading role in defining motivation for typical behavior patterns. Another way of organizing the nine types into three groups is to consider three patterns of engaging with projects or people, called Process Styles. (Names for these groupings vary among Enneagram teachers. I have chosen to use language that is consistent with business applications.) There are three types within each of the three Process Styles. Types Three, Seven, and Eight are known as the Initiator types. Their style of engagement is to bring a lot of energy and enthusiasm to projects, taking the lead (or initiative) and preferring to get started and learn while doing. I have called this the "Ready-Fire-Aim" group. They are most comfortable with trying things out, making a few mistakes and using the new information to guide the further development of the enterprise. They may shoot a few arrows in the general direction of the target to find the strategy that best hits the target, then refine the aim. While they may waste some resources, they tend to get things done and not get bogged down with difficult details or obstacles. They are often ambitious and find themselves in top leadership roles.

A second group is called Cooperators, not because they are necessarily cooperative with other people, but because they cooperate with the rules as they understand and define them. This group includes Types One, Two, and Six. They are not happy jumping right into a project, but want to spell out the expectations, the rules or guidelines, the details about roles and deadline BEFORE the work actually begins. They are what I call the "Ready-Aim, Aim, Aim-Fire" group.

The utility described earlier is a regulated industry and compliance with the rules is essential to the continued operation of the company. It is in the best interest of leaders, most of whom are Initiators, to allow their managers and Cooperator colleagues to manage this aspect of the business.

The last sub-group is called Soloists and includes Types Four, Five and Nine. Individuals in this group tend to show up at meetings, but appear not to fully engage until they have had time to digest the scope of the project and what is expected of them before emerging to discuss their contribution. They take longer to engage. Others may mistake their typical pattern as lack of cooperation but it is only a preferred style to allow them to get a clear internal sense of direction. I call them the "Ready, ready, ready-Aim-Fire" group because though they may seem slow in starting, once they feel ready they can be productive and enthusiastic contributors.

We also use the process style grouping of the nine types to talk about how individuals function and influence performance within a team environment. The nine types are grouped into three team roles. We are assuming that all of these roles are important to high-functioning teams. When assigning people to a team, it is important to explicitly consider type in addition to specific professional acumen and skills to ensure that the team works effectively. We will discuss this use of team roles in the application section below.

Another grouping of types gives leaders essential information to guide their organizations when things do not go according to plan. These are called Conflict styles and senior leaders do not tend to cluster in only one of these groups. The first pattern or style of managing conflict is to catalyze the potential conflict brewing under the surface, to identify it, name it, and bring it out in the open with all the emotion that can be attached to conflicting, frustrating, or disappointing situations. The downside to this approach is that perceived potential conflicts may not be real and a lot of emotional energy may be discharged that does not serve the group's purpose. Types Eight, Six, and Four are in this group.

Another pattern or approach is called the competency style in which once a real problem is identified these types want to prove their competence by focusing all of their resources on addressing the issue until it is resolved. Emotion is set aside in service to achieving the goals. However, given that problems are inevitable and ongoing within any organization this approach keeps people in a driven mode that can burn them out. The third group uses the Positive Attitude approach by keeping people in touch with the big picture so they are not discouraged. The motto for the Positive Attitude group is: "Don't sweat the small stuff." In an effort to stay optimistic, however, they may sometimes overlook details or issues that are not, in fact, small stuff and that need attention. Types Seven, Two and Nine are in this group.

Putting these three groupings of three types into a table we have an easy way to organize Enneagram information. In selecting people for teams, it is important to have all three process types (initiators, cooperators, and soloists) represented. The diversity of types ensures that all key roles are covered. Because each type has different strengths and talents that create a comprehensive solution and strong execution, teams that are relatively homogeneous are much less likely to navigate complex change successfully.

Table 1.3

HOW DO YOU LIKE TO WORK?			
	INITIATORS	COOPERATORS	SOLOISTS
How do you cope when there are problems?	Like to get started and learn as they go along. They like action, diving in, getting engaged, and being involved	Want to take time to find out who the team is, understand the framework and what is behind it, and clarify expectations, rules, and guidelines in more detail. They have more questions about who is in charge of what and explore potential conflict with differing expectations	Want to spend some time independently thinking about a situation and feeling their way to an inner understanding of it. Others may perceive them as being withdrawn to the exclusion of others, or even being aloof
Positive outlook style	Type Seven- The Enthusiast. Joyful Visionary: Optimistic, energetic. Can become scattered or bored	Type Two- The Helper. Thoughtful Contributor: Alert to others' needs. Can become a self-important busybody	Type Nine- The Mediator. Comforting Optimist: Can see all sides and help find compromise. Can become a passive wishful thinker

Competency style	Type Three- The Achiever Competent Pragmatist: Wants results and to be successful Can value image over substance	Type One- The Reformer Conscientious Teacher: Attends to details and wants to get it right Can become a rigid scorekeeper	Type Five- The Analyst Perceptive Expert: Organizes data well, out-of-box thinking Can become a detached technician
Catalyst style	Type Eight- The Challenger Self-Confident Authority: Visionary, assertive leadership Can become a heavy-handed taskmaster	Type Six- The Loyalist Dependable Associate: Hard-working, loyal, a good team player Can be a worrier, focusing on worst-case scenarios	Type Four- The Individualist Intuitive Originator: Creative, tuned in to emotions Can be crippled by inner emotional conflicts, temperamental and withholding

Summary

Good leaders are like conductors of an orchestra. The conductor knows the overall piece of music and all of the individual parts, but does not actually play an instrument in the performance. Instead he provides the tempo, keeps all the musicians in balance, and allows each performer to contribute his best to the overall performance. Understanding his own style, he can communicate it to the orchestra to prepare them for how they will be asked to work together. Understanding other styles, he helps all the parts work together as a whole to accomplish something none of them could do alone.

In summary, by harnessing the capacity to see your Leader Type and conditioning in an objective, nonjudgmental way, you are able to foster better insight in relation to your own experience without the strained effort that can stem from self-bias. You discovered that the unique patterns that shape each type are genuine, natural, and generally do not change much over time. In the most basic way, they simply reflect who you are most innately. The goal with Leader Type is to build self-awareness and leverage strengths, not try to change who you are. Understanding the natural conditioning that comes from Leader Type is a crucial stage in developing leadership effectiveness and comprehensive innovation within the entire organization.

REFLECTION QUESTIONS

Based on this chapter and using the Enneagram numbers, what type do you think you might be?

━━━━━━━

Have you used other typing tools in the past? How?

━━━━━━━

Does the information about type help increase your level of awareness regarding your habitual patterns, strengths, and growth opportunities?

━━━━━━━

Do you use this type-based information to guide how you interact with others?

━━━━━━━

Would an increased use of type knowledge help improve your team effectiveness by promoting discussion among team members about preferred roles and communication styles?

Enneagram Quick Reference Page

This summary page provides you with a place to capture your scores, and notes about yourself and your type. In the column "Your Score," indicate what percentage of your personality falls into each category with the total being 100% You can detach and use it as you read this chapter, or retain it in the book for future reference.

Table 1.4

TYPE	Name	Characteristics	Your Score	Your Notes
One	Reformer	Rational, principled, self-controlled		
Two	Helper	Caring, generous, possessive		
Three	Achiever	Adaptable, ambitious, image-conscious		
Four	Individualist	Intuitive, aesthetic, self-absorbed		
Five	Investigator	Perceptive, innovative, detached		
Six	Loyalist	Engaging, responsible, defensive		
Seven	Enthusiast	Upbeat, accomplished, impulsive		
Eight	Challenger	Self-confident, decisive, domineering		
Nine	Peacemaker	Receptive, reassuring, complacent		
TOTAL			100%	

CHAPTER 2
Developmental Perspectives

Fig. 2.1 Five Elements of Innovative Leadership

Leadership Behaviors

Situational Analysis

Resilience

Developmental Perspective

Leader Type

In the previous chapter, we explored how to apply an understanding of your type to leadership. We started by simply examining the patterns that comprise your type and serve as a foundation for both personal and professional transformation. We then used these types to evaluate the leadership culture of the organization. We will now shift from type to Developmental Perspective and discuss how it supports your success in transforming your organization.

The Importance of Developmental Perspective

In this guide we will be talking about **Developmental Perspectives** as a key element in applying innovative leadership. Developmental perspectives significantly influence how you see your role and function in the workplace, how you interact with others, and how you solve problems. The term "Developmental Perspective" can be described as "meaning making" or how you make sense of experiences. This is important because the algorithm you use to make sense of the world influences your thoughts and actions. Incorporating these perspectives as part of your interactions with others will improve your success as you lead a transformation effort.

As an innovative leader, developing yourself isn't enough. You must also have an ability to understand others through the developmental lens and relate to them using Developmental Perspective as an important filter for interactions. This will inform the staffing selections you make, the roles you and others take within teams, and groups, and the language and communication style you use when interacting with others in all settings. When working with Developmental Perspective, it is important to remember that we work with this concept so we can be more effective in our interaction with others. There are not better or worse levels; there are, however, better fits and worse fits. When making selections, we look at level like we do skill. You are not selected for a job for which you do not have the appropriate skills. Instead, we add another criterion: Developmental Perspective. When selecting people for your change effort, it will be important to consider skills and match of Developmental Perspective to the role. We map Developmental Perspective to rules just as we map skills and make selections based on both criteria.

One of the characteristics of the Developmental Perspective model we believe is most important is the layout of a natural and logical path for growth. While people move through these perspectives (levels) at different rates following a relatively predictable path, performance can be bolstered by understanding the needs at each perspective. Many adults will become more effective within their level without actually moving up a level or adding a perspective. Helping leaders move to later, more expansive (higher) developmental levels is also important to increasing organizational success. Development can be accelerated by creating an organizational culture that supports it. For this reason, by understanding the developmental process and perspectives, the pitfalls, and the enablers, you will be able to create an organization that supports development so that your leaders that can effectively foster transformation efforts.

Because the concept of Developmental Perspectives is often overlooked in mainstream organizational literature and programs and because we believe it is critical to effectively transforming organizations, we're intentionally giving it a lot of attention. We'll look at the six most common of those meaning-making approaches in greater detail; then, we will talk about how to use this concept when transforming your organization.

Fig. 2.2 Enneagram & Developmental Perspectives

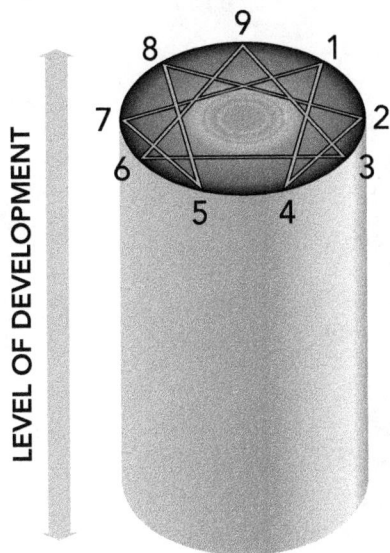

In order to connect Developmental Perspective with Leader Type, let's look at how these models come together. While Leader Type is generally constant, you have the capacity to grow and develop your leadership perspective. In fact, leadership research strongly suggests that although inherent Leader Type determines your tendency to lead, good leaders develop over time. Therefore, it is often the case that leaders are perhaps both born *and* made. How leaders are made is best described using an approach that considers Developmental Perspective. Type remains consistent during your life while Developmental Perspective grows and is an important differentiator in leadership effectiveness.

This model helps us clarify how leaders develop individually; it also applies to the organizational level to help select and train leaders more effectively. Here are some additional benefits of using a model of Developmental Perspective:

- It guides leaders in determining their personal development goals and action plans by helping leaders understand the next step in either enhancing their abilities at the current perspective or gaining access to the next perspective.

- It is a tool when determining which individuals and team members best fit specific roles considering skill and Developmental Perspective.

- It helps in identifying which high-potential leaders to groom for growth opportunities.

- It can be used in creating interview questions in the hiring process that illuminate the key behaviors required for success in the job.

- It helps change agents understand the perspective of change targets and craft solutions that meet the needs of all stakeholders.

The Leadership Maturity Model and Developmental Levels / Perspectives

Fig. 2.3 Maslow's Hierarchy of Needs

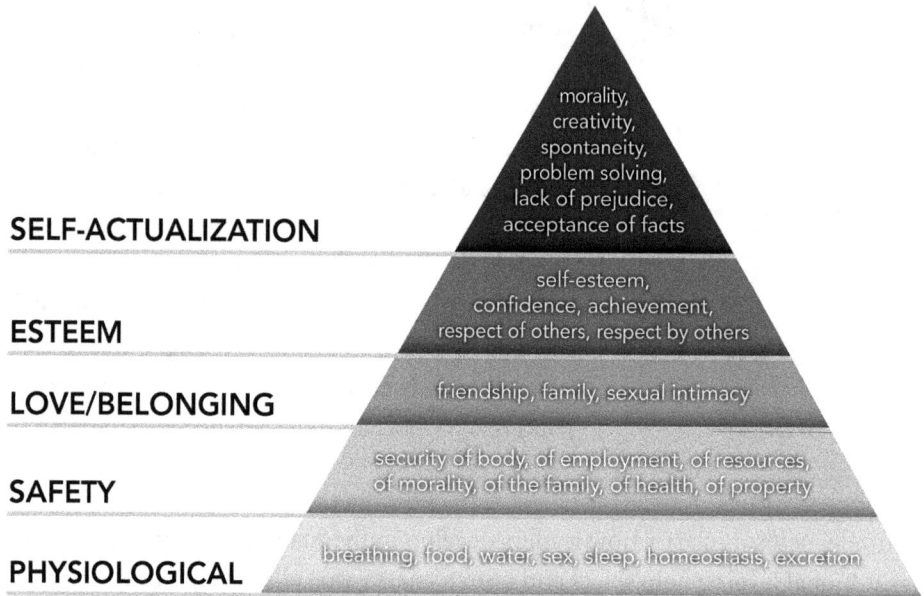

SELF-ACTUALIZATION — morality, creativity, spontaneity, problem solving, lack of prejudice, acceptance of facts

ESTEEM — self-esteem, confidence, achievement, respect of others, respect by others

LOVE/BELONGING — friendship, family, sexual intimacy

SAFETY — security of body, of employment, of resources, of morality, of the family, of health, of property

PHYSIOLOGICAL — breathing, food, water, sex, sleep, homeostasis, excretion

The Developmental Perspective approach is based on research and observation that, over time, people tend to grow and progress through a number of very distinct stages of awareness and ability. One of the most well-known and tested developmental models is Abraham Maslow's *hierarchy of needs*—a pyramid visual aid Maslow created to help explain his theory of levels of human needs, both psychological and physical. As you ascend the steps of the pyramid you can eventually reach a level of self-actualization.

Developmental growth occurs much like other capabilities grow in your life. Building on your Leader Type, you continue to grow, increasing access to or capacity for additional skills. We call this "transcend and include" in that you transcend the prior level, or perspective, and still maintain the ability to function at that perspective. Let us use the example of learning how to run to illustrate the process of development. You must first learn to stand and walk before you can run. And yet, as you eventually master running, you still effortlessly retain the earlier, foundational skill that allowed you to stand and walk. In other words, you can develop your capacity to build beyond the basic skills you have now by moving through more progressive stages.

People develop through stages at vastly differing rates, often influenced by significant events or "disorienting dilemmas." Those events or dilemmas provide opportunities to begin experiencing your world from a completely different point-of-view. The nature of those influential events can vary greatly, ranging from positive social occasions like marriage, a new job, or the birth of a child, to negative experiences, such as job loss, an accident, or death of a loved one. These situations may often trigger more lasting changes in your way of thinking and feeling. New Developmental Perspectives can develop very gradually over time or, in some cases, transpire quite abruptly.

Some developmentally advanced people may be relatively young while others may experience very little developmental growth over the course of a lifetime. Adding to the complexity of developmental growth is that the unfolding of Developmental Perspectives is not predictably evident along the lines of age, gender, nationality, or affluence. We can only experientially sense indicators that help us identify Developmental Perspective when we listen and exchange ideas with others, employ introspection, and display openness to learning. In fact, most people very naturally intuit and discern what motivates others as well as what causes some of their greatest challenges.

To further examine Developmental Perspectives we use the **Maturity Assessment Profile (MAP)** and its conceptual support, the **Leadership Maturity Framework (LMF)** assessment tools. This developmental toolset was created by Susanne Cook-Greuter as part of her doctoral dissertation at Harvard, and we use them as the foundation for our developmental discussion.

The MAP delivers practical information that can be translated into an actionable development plan. This instrument is the most rigorously developed Harvard-tested, unbiased, and reliable perspective measure on the market. The MAP provides unique and personal feedback in addition to perspective description and score. The MAP is also the most sophisticated instrument for identifying and measuring later stage, developmentally advanced leadership. The MAP evaluates three primary dimensions to determine Developmental Perspective: cognitive complexity, emotional competence, and behavior.

Table 2.1

THREE DIMENSIONS OF DEVELOPMENTAL LEVEL

- **Cognitive complexity** describes your capacity to take multiple perspectives and think through increasingly more complex problems. This is akin to solving an algebra problem with multiple variables. For example, a complex thinker is able to balance competing interests like employees' desire for higher pay, with customers' desire to pay low prices and receive good service

- **Emotional competence** describes your self-awareness, self-management, awareness of others, and your ability to build and maintain effective relationships, along with your capacity for empathetic response

- **Behavior** generally describes the actions you take

A sense of time, or time horizon, is another essential feature in the development of perspective. For example, if a leader is limited by his Developmental Perspective to thinking about the completion of tasks within a timeline of three months or less, then optimally he should only be leading a part of the organization that requires short-term tasks. On the other hand, if a leader has the capacity to think and implement tasks with three-year time horizons, then that leader can and likely should be taking on a role that includes longer-term tasks. This could be a leader responsible for overseeing the implementation of an enterprise-wide computer system where the migration may take substantially more time and the process is more complex.

Elaborating on this example, there will be components of the team primarily responsible for the more tactical, hands-on part of the installation who demonstrate shorter time horizon thinking. Obviously, they are held accountable for certain tasks within the plan but will not be responsible for designing the more strategic portions, nor be charged with the daily decisions that impact the overall budget.

Further still, imagine that one year into the project a key member of the team takes another job and the project manager (PM) becomes responsible for finding a suitable replacement. The project manager must consider all options when selecting a replacement. The most effective staffing solution for the project will need to account for potential changes over the next two years and how the replacement will impact overall project cost, quality of the final outcome, and team cohesiveness. Time horizons, along with developmental complexity, are directly applicable to innovative organizational decisions.

Detailed Review of Developmental Perspectives

In this section we'll examine the six Developmental Perspectives most often found in leadership roles. We will also explore an example of a leader as she develops through some of those Developmental Perspectives while her underlying type remains unchanged. The following table reflects percentages of leaders testing at each perspective from the David Rooke and Bill Torbert article, "Seven Transformations of Leadership" in the *Harvard Business Review*. We provided a Developmental Perspective quick reference card at the end of this chapter for you to capture your own score and notes as you read the chapter.

Table 2.2

DESCRIPTION OF DEVELOPMENTAL LEVELS / PERSPECTIVES	% of Sample
Diplomat ▪ Demonstrates predominately concrete thinking style ▪ Hyper-concerned with social acceptance ▪ Emphasis on conforming to the rules and norms of the desired group ▪ Imagines that others think and feel the same as they do	12%
Expert ▪ Demonstrates basic abstract thinking ▪ Concerned with expressing a sense of individuality in sharp contrast to others ▪ Concerned with measuring up to the "right" standards ▪ Can often appear to be a perfectionist ▪ Makes constant comparisons with others to gauge identity ▪ Can often be critical and blame-oriented ▪ Adept at developing multiple new solutions to problems but not able to determine the best fit solution ▪ Can begin envisioning short-term time horizons: three months to one year	38%
Achiever ▪ Basic ability to identify shades of grey and see conceptual complexity ▪ Focuses on causes, achievement, and effectiveness ▪ Considers others while pursuing their own individual agendas and ideas ▪ Sees themselves as part of the larger group, yet separate and responsible for their own choices ▪ Appreciates mutual expression of differences ▪ Time horizon one to five years	30%

Individualist - Increased capacity for advanced complex thinking - Exhibits an ability to appreciate paradox in circumstances - Begins to value and use rudimentary aspects of intuition - Beginning awareness that perception shapes reality, including their own - Self-reflective and investigative of their own personalized assumptions, as well as those of others - Understands mutual interdependence with others - Lives personal convictions according to internal standards - Interest in feedback becomes very important - Longer time horizon: five to ten years - Tend to move into change agent/consultant/portfolio roles	**10%**
Strategist - Perceives systematic patterns and long-term trends with uncanny clarity - Can easily differentiate objective versus subjective biased events - Exhibits a strong focus on self-development, self-actualization, and authenticity - Pursues actualizing personal convictions according to internal standards - Management style is tenacious, yet humble - Understands the importance of mutual interdependence with others - Integrating feedback into performance is very important - Tend to move into change agent/consultant/portfolio roles - Well-advanced time horizon: approximately fifteen to twenty years with concern for legacy	**4%**
Magician / Alchemist - Seeks transformation of organizations not according to conventional goals but according to a higher order - Has a transforming ability to draw together opposites and initiate new directions from creative tension - Tends to build their own novel organizations or work on their own to offer their best contribution to humanity - Seen as visionary leaders - May lead from behind, or in a more subtle way - Time horizon in excess of twenty years	**1%**

Developmental Perspective and Organizational Effectiveness

Developmental perspective not only helps you as an individual leader create your growth path, it is also important in transforming your organization. The key to high performance is to align people and roles considering their Developmental Perspective. Different functions within the organization are best filled by people at different Developmental Perspectives. We call this their "fit" for the role, or more precisely, how the qualities associated with their Developmental Perspective align with requirements specific to the job. It is important for both leaders and organizations to support the health of all employees from a developmental standpoint and create an environment where each individual is in a role where he best fits and can move toward achieving his fullest potential.

In order for you to be successful as a leader over the long run, it is essential to understand your proper "fit" within the organization—which includes understanding who you are and what you value, where you belong in the organization, and where you belong within the broader team and community stakeholders. It is also important to apply this concept to others as you are making hiring decisions, assigning people to roles, determining individual roles within a team, and communicating with others. Importantly, the goal is not merely to build an organization with all people at the "highest" Developmental Perspective, rather it is to select people for roles that allow them to function as effectively as possible individually and collectively. ***Your organization will be effective if it supports success for people at all levels and aligns them to roles that fit their capacity.*** Organizations that perceive one perspective as "better" will be less effective than organizations that leverage every perspective and design an organization where all levels can thrive concurrently and are working toward a collective goal of organizational success using a broad range of skills and perspectives.

You can use this developmental model with organizations in several ways:

- Make staffing and succession decisions using Developmental Perspectives. Consider Developmental Perspective along with past performance and technical and industry skills, align people to the roles that have the best "fit."

- Improve communication skills by applying a general understanding of Developmental Perspective to guide leaders in improving interpersonal effectiveness. Instead of simply communicating with others as ourselves, we recommend communicating with them based on their perspective. Understanding the perceptions of others from a developmental standpoint can dramatically improve interpersonal effectiveness. This is true with staff, peers, bosses, clients, family members, as well as other stakeholders.

- Improve management and leadership by applying an understanding of Developmental Perspectives allowing a leader to clarify the needs of employees. For example, **Expert** employees want clear and specific directions and guidelines so they can do their tasks "right." **Individualists** want the freedom to determine the best approach to accomplishing tasks. Trying to manage these different Developmental Perspectives using the same approach will result in frustration and lost productivity.

- Comparing the organizational developmental level to your personal developmental level will help you better understand the organizational culture. Organizations develop along the same trajectory as people: they start with the need to establish basic rules and infrastructure, and then move to more complex functioning as they progress through the organizational lifecycle. Understanding the culture will help you because, as an innovative leader, you are continually aligning your intentions and behaviors with the culture and systems of the organization. While we do not address organizational maturity in this book, if you are interested in learning more, you may reference *Action Inquiry: The Secret of Timely and Transforming Leadership* by Bill Torbert.

Application

Dan is working as the general manager of an organization within a large government system. Dan's tests show him as a Strategist. His organization is experiencing major change because of political realignment after a scandal. His organization may transition from government operated to a nongovernmental agency in the near future in response to the realignment.

The following table gives a few examples of the challenges Dan faced with his team and solutions he developed as he became more familiar with how to apply his understanding of Developmental Perspectives. It is important to note that he did not "test" his staff but rather developed his own ability to generally evaluate them. This rough estimate gave him enough information to refine how he worked with people. I do want to be clear that you can only know the perspectives by doing a true assessment. For Dan's purposes, having a rough understanding gave him the information he needed to navigate the transformation he was implementing.

Dan acted in a manner that was highly ethical with this information. He did not use it to pigeon hole or marginalize people in any way. This assessment, like any other assessment tool that puts people into categories, can be used "against" or "for" people based on the criteria. We are talking about only using it to improve how we interact with people based on their perspective, not withholding promotions or denying people in any way. We do not use it as a sole hiring tool although we do use our understanding of the criteria to develop interview questions that will help identify fit for the job based on Developmental Perspective.

The following table shows some of the challenges Dan faced, how these challenges can be seen through a developmental lens, and the solutions he devised based on his knowledge of Developmental Perspectives. He found this lens to be very helpful and it gave him a valuable tool to think through many of the challenges he had been facing over the past years. Our exploration of Developmental Perspective illustrates that having a deep understanding of perspectives is a critical element when transforming an organization. Understanding this element of leadership gives you a powerful tool to successfully implement transformation in response to adaptive challenges. It will help you identify and reduce frustration, and increase employee engagement.

Table 2.3

Challenge	Developmental Lesson	Solution
Asked people for **input on large strategic issues** and learned that many people on his staff really did not want to provide input. They wanted him to set the course and they would determine how to implement his plan within their individual departments	Many of his staff operate at the **Expert** level and, at that perspective, people want the boss to set the direction. The Expert might say something like: *How should I know how to proceed? That's what he's paid to figure out—not me. Even worse, they could say: If he doesn't know where we're going, then he's an incompetent boss and we should not follow him*	Realize that people at different levels will have different expectations about organizational roles. For a staff that is predominantly Expert, the leader needs to take a more active role in setting direction and ask for input at the **Task** level, not the **Strategic** level

Challenge	Developmental Lesson	Solution
Giving direction on organizational changes and <u>job or task changes</u>	His team members at the **Individualist** and **Strategist** levels want people to make suggestions about high level goals and step back to allow them to figure out how to accomplish the result His **Achievers** simply want to know the desired outcome and some general guidelines and measures—then they go to work. They want to know how they will be evaluated and who they are competing with so they could start the competition The **Experts** work better when told how to accomplish the task. Because they want to do the job right, it is important to clarify what "right" looks like. In a transformation project this could look like very clearly defined operating procedures and "day in the life" scenarios	Understand the perspective of those being asked to change and craft the materials accordingly. For jobs within the organization that primarily involve concrete tasks and a "right and wrong" way to do them, it is important to provide clearly documented procedures and support materials so the employee can understand and perform well. Jobs that are more conceptual and are not generally defined by a clear right and wrong answer are usually performed by people with later level Developmental Perspectives and they respond best to general guidelines for the expected outcome rather than the step-by-step process about how to accomplish the assignment

Challenge	Developmental Lesson	Solution
Amount and type of **information shared**	His **Individualists** are more concerned with involvement, inclusion, and ensuring that the broader community is being served by the mission. They want to reach consensus on issues that are important to them. This range of concerns and communication styles can make a simple staff meeting frustrating for everyone involved His **Achievers** are most concerned with accomplishing results and do not care so much about who is coming and going, or why, as long as they have what they need to accomplish their goals. They want quick answers so they can get back to the activities at hand and make things happen His **Experts** are very concerned with equity and fairness. To them, it is not fair if someone comes in late or leaves early when he is on vacation and not "watching them." They want the boss to be in charge and make decisions	If the meeting is to gain consensus on an important issue, allow time for conversation and clarify the process by which decisions will be reached (time box the conversation according to the importance of the issue) If the meeting is to share status, send clear reports in advance and structure the meeting to share information that is important for the group to know. Only invite people who are impacted by the information and allow the balance of the group to focus on the results they are trying to accomplish. Collaboration and information sharing are often critical and can be very time consuming. Determine the most efficient approach given the culture and still focus on results Structure meetings using clear agendas and processes to accomplish stated outcomes. If the goal to share information is non-negotiable, structure the meeting accordingly

Challenge	Developmental Lesson	Solution
Assign (hire) people to roles based on job related skills and also developmental level	People with great self-awareness and interpersonal skills are often promoted to executive roles and they may prefer inclusion and developing people over accomplishing the mission People with great skills in managing people to get things done are promoted to senior leadership roles and are often not inclined to slow down and consider longer-term implications and interconnection of consequences for their decisions People who perform well in individual contributor roles are often promoted to supervisory roles for which they are ill equipped lacking the interpersonal skills to supervise and manage	When hiring for key roles, evaluate not only the job skills, but also the Developmental Perspective to successfully perform the role By expanding hiring criteria, you can avoid some time consuming and costly pitfalls that adversely impact organizational health and success If you are interested in considering Developmental Perspective when hiring, you can create behavioral interview questions or scenarios that will test the thinking process and behavior of a leader in specific settings. While this will not tell you his Developmental Perspective, it will tell if he has access to the thinking and behavior you are seeking to be successful in the specific role

This chapter provided a brief introduction of a Developmental Perspective model and gives an example of how it can be applied. It is helpful for you to understand your own Developmental Perspective and also have a sense of the perspectives of those around you. You will not be testing everyone in the organization, but will have a sense of levels of key jobs or roles within the organization and use this understanding as input when designing your transformation initiative. It is important to note that you do not need precise scores, but often simply a general sense of people will help you quickly improve your effectiveness in dealing with them. Understanding how to apply this model effectively can greatly improve your communication effectiveness and interpersonal interactions with people who function at different perspectives.

REFLECTION QUESTIONS

Based on this chapter, where would you place yourself on the developmental level/perspective continuum?

━━━━━━

Given your current job, is your Developmental Perspective a good fit with your role?

━━━━━━

As you read Dan's story, could you identify two or three people in your life who function at different perspectives? Given this brief summary, how might you interact with them differently to increase your collective effectiveness?

━━━━━━

Does this understanding of Developmental Perspective give you helpful information about how to work with different groups of people during your transformation effort?

━━━━━━

How can you include your understanding of Developmental Perspective into your hiring decisions by mapping Developmental Perspective to each key role?

━━━━━━

Can you roughly identify Developmental Perspective of your key employees and prepare for important discussions by designing the conversational tone and content around what the recipient of the information can best understand and integrate?

Developmental Perspective Quick Reference Page

This summary page provides you with a place to capture your scores, and notes about yourself and your Developmental Perspective. You can detach and use it as you read this chapter, or retain it in the book for future reference.

With the Enneagram, we provided a reference to a free assessment. We aren't aware of a similar assessment free of charge for Developmental Perspective, but we believe you can approximate your Developmental Perspective relatively accurately. We encourage you to capture what percentage of your development is reflected by each level. In other words, how much of your day is spent acting from the point of view of a diplomat? An expert?

Table 2.4

Description of Developmental Levels / Perspectives	Your Score	Your Notes
Diplomat - Demonstrates predominately concrete thinking style - Hyper-concerned with social acceptance - Emphasis on conforming to the rules and norms of the desired group - Imagines that others think and feel the same as they do		
Expert - Demonstrates basic abstract thinking - Concerned with expressing a sense of individuality in sharp contrast to others - Concerned with measuring up to the "right" standards - Can often appear to be a perfectionist - Makes constant comparisons with others to gauge identity - Can often be critical and blame-oriented - Adept at developing multiple new solutions to problems but not able to determine the best fit solution - Can begin envisioning short-term time horizons: three months to one year		

Description of Developmental Levels / Perspectives	Your Score	Your Notes
Achiever - Basic ability to identify shades of grey and see conceptual complexity - Focuses on causes, achievement, and effectiveness - Considers others while pursuing their own individual agendas and ideas - Sees themselves as part of the larger group, yet separate and responsible for their own choices - Appreciates mutual expression of differences - Time horizon: one to five-years		
Individualist - Increased capacity for advanced complex thinking - Exhibits an ability to appreciate paradox in circumstances - Begins to value and use rudimentary aspects of intuition - Beginning awareness that perception shapes reality, including their own - Self-reflective and investigative of their own personalized assumptions, as well as those of others - Understands mutual interdependence with others - Lives personal convictions according to internal standards - Interest in feedback becomes very important - Longer time horizon: five to ten years - Tend to move into change agent/consultant/ portfolio roles		

Description of Developmental Levels / Perspectives	Your Score	Your Notes
Strategist - Perceives systematic patterns and long-term trends with uncanny clarity - Can easily differentiate objective versus subjective biased events - Exhibits a strong focus on self-development, self-actualization, and authenticity - Pursues actualizing personal convictions according to internal standards - Management style is tenacious, yet humble - Understands the importance of mutual interdependence with others - Integrating feedback into performance is very important - Tend to move into change agent/consultant/ portfolio roles - Well-advanced time horizon: approximately fifteen to twenty years with concern for legacy		
Magician / Alchemist - Seeks transformation of organizations not according to conventional goals but according to a higher order - Has a transforming ability to draw together opposites and initiate new directions from creative tension - Tends to build their own novel organizations or work on their own to offer their best contribution to humanity - Seen as visionary leaders - May lead from behind, or in a more subtle way - Time horizon: in excess of twenty years		
TOTAL	100%	

CHAPTER 3
Resilience

Fig. 3.1 Five Elements of Innovative Leadership

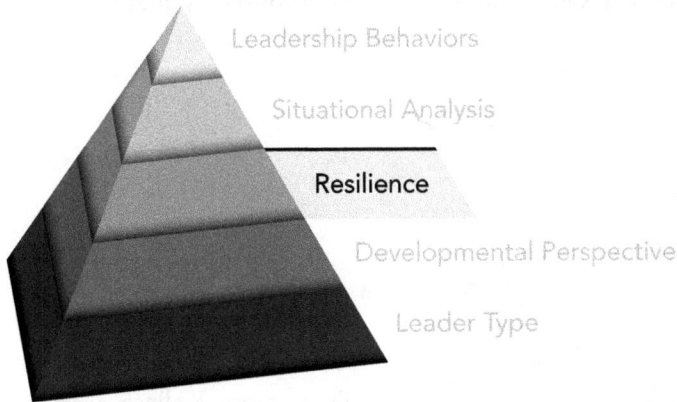

Leadership Behaviors

Situational Analysis

Resilience

Developmental Perspective

Leader Type

In previous chapters, we introduced the qualities that comprise your Leader Type and the potential you have to enhance your Developmental Perspective. In examining Resilience, we are going to further explore the physical and psychological nuances of both Leader Type and Developmental Perspective and how they impact individual and organizational well-being. The underlying premise is this: as a leader, you need to be physically and emotionally healthy to do a good job. In addition to physical and emotional health, the resilient leader also has a clear sense of life purpose and strong supportive relationships. Organizations need to consist of healthy people—and that happens when the leaders, culture, systems, and processes promote health during times of stress. For most people and organizations, enhancing resilience requires a personal change.

There are two distinct ways to understand Resilience. First, *from a leadership perspective*, resilience can be viewed as the ability to adapt in the face of ongoing change while continuing to be both fluid in approach and driven toward attaining strategic goals. Second, *from a systems perspective*, using an engineering analogy, resilience is viewed as how much disturbance your systems can absorb before a breakdown. This view highlights the sturdiness of systems which could be something like a bridge or a larger system like an organizational system or environmental system. The first refers to fluidity and endurance while the second reflects stability. Addressing all aspects of Resilience is critical when transforming an organization.

The Importance of Resilience

Among the elements essential to leadership, Resilience is unique in that it integrates the physical and psychological aspects of Leader Type and Developmental Perspective to create the foundation of a leader's inner stability. This foundation enables you to demonstrate fluidity and endurance as you appropriately adapt to ongoing change.

The Resilience Model

Fig. 3.2 Elements of Resilience

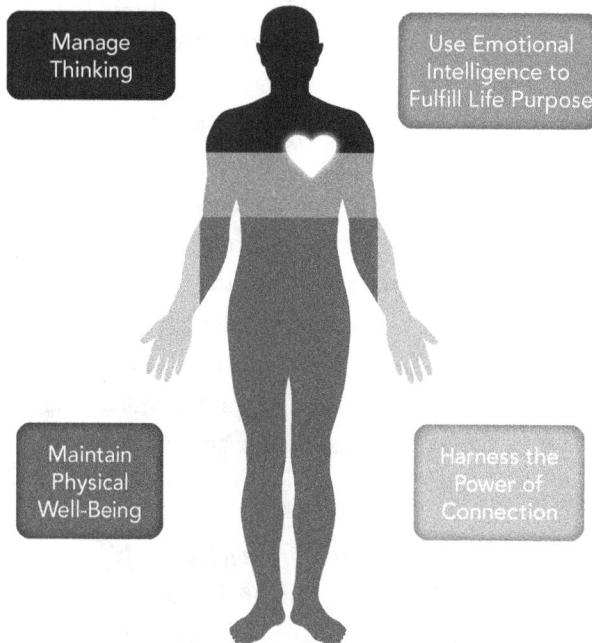

Manage Thinking

Use Emotional Intelligence to Fulfill Life Purpose

Maintain Physical Well-Being

Harness the Power of Connection

Our Resilience approach is based on research by Dr. Suzanne Kobasa, as well as current business research from organizations such as Gallup that investigate well-being, and the Human Performance Institute that focuses on the corporate athlete.

Our model has four categories, shown in Figure 3.2. They are: Maintain Physical Well-being, Manage Thinking, Use Emotional Intelligence to Fulfill Life Purpose, and Harness the Power of Connection. These categories are interlinked and, consistent with leading research, must all be in balance to create long-term resilience.

Leaders we work with often say they are too busy to take care of themselves. There is a balance between self-care and meeting all of our daily commitments. Most leaders fall short of their own personal resilience goals and make daily choices for personal health or against it. Our message here is that creating and maintaining Resilience is essential to your success. As you improve your Resilience, you will think more clearly and have a greater positive impact in your interactions with others; investing in your personal resilience supports the entire organization's effectiveness.

In an organizational transformation, it is critical to devote as much time to leader behaviors that promote Resilience as well as to culture and organizational systems and processes. To build a truly resilient organization, leaders must make deliberate choices about building resilience into key systems and processes, and modeling behaviors that demonstrate the importance of it. Most organizations in the United States do not sufficiently promote Resilience while many European companies, based on their culture and systems, have elements that promote building a resilient workforce. While we are interested in studying the variances between countries, this book does not provide additional examination.

Table 3.1 provides keys to building and retaining personal Resilience. To promote Resilience, organizations must support and reinforce these behaviors. If you are interested in learning more about your personal Resilience, you can take a free Resilience exercise at www.metcalf-associates.com. You will find a Resilience Quick Reference Page at the end of this chapter.

Table 3.1

KEYS TO BUILDING & RETAINING PERSONAL RESILIENCE	
Manage Thinking Practice telling yourself: - Challenges are normal and healthy for any individual or organization - My current problem is a doorway to an innovative solution - I feel inspired about the opportunity to create new possibilities that did not exist before	**Use Emotional Intelligence to Fulfill Life Purpose** Understand what you stand for. Maintain focus. Ask: - What is my purpose? - Why is it important to me? - What values do I hold that will enable me to accomplish my purpose? - What opportunities do I have in my professional life that help me to achieve my life purpose?
Maintain Physical Well-Being Are you getting enough: - Sleep - Exercise - Healthy food - Time in nature - Time to meditate and relax Are you limiting or eliminating: - Caffeine - Nicotine	**Harness the Power of Connection** Practice effective communication: - Say things simply and clearly - Make communication safe by being responsive - Encourage people to ask questions and clarify if they do not understand your message - Balance advocacy for your point with inquiring about the other person's points - When you have a different point of view, seek to understand how and why the other person believes what they do in a non-threatening way - When in doubt, share information and emotions - Build trust by acting for the greater good

Maintain Physical Well-Being

According to Gallup, "Those with high physical well-being simply have more energy to get more done in less time. You are more likely to be in a good mood, thus boosting the engagement of your colleagues and customers."

Physical well-being is something you likely understand and yet give limited focus. Some basic elements include:

- Get enough sleep
- Exercise six days per week
- Eat well
- Limit caffeine and alcohol
- Eliminate nicotine
- Meditate and relax
- Take time in nature

While the need for sleep may seem obvious, on a regular basis many people still work with a sleep deficit. There is an increasing body of research supporting the idea that you are less effective when sleep deprived. Additionally, while there is conflicting data, more research suggests that it is important to exercise six days per week including aerobics and strength training. Other studies also point to the strong positive impact of meditation and other stress reduction approaches such as Mindfulness Based Stress Reduction (MBSR) programs. In a study that appeared in the January 30, 2011, issue of *Psychiatry Research: Neuroimaging*, "A team led by Massachusetts General Hospital (MGH) researchers report the results of their study, the first to document meditation-produced changes over time in the brain's grey matter... Participating in an 8-week mindfulness meditation program appears to make measurable changes in brain regions associated with memory, sense of self, empathy and [reduced] stress."

One of the goals in maintaining physical well-being is managing the amount and impact of stress. We define stress as one of several physical or emotional factors that create physiological and/or psychological tension. Tension is normal and adaptive when the autonomic nervous system processes it in a healthy manner. Problems occur only if you do not recover from tension quickly, leading to symptoms caused by reduced immune system functioning.

___Key to physical well-being___: Build daily routines that help your body recover from stress.

The physiological impact of ongoing stress is often debilitating because of the negative impact on your body's immune system. If your body is not given regular opportunities to recover from tension associated with stress, the results can range from diminished concentration to anxiety and/or depression to vulnerability to disease, including chronic conditions.

Manage Thinking

Your mental perspective is based on your attitudes, beliefs, and assumptions rather than knowledge. It is essential to stay in touch with what is really happening now instead of limiting yourself with beliefs and assumptions based on your past experiences which may no longer be relevant. Assumptions can diminish your capacity for awareness by holding on to prior beliefs that you think are still true, and negative and inflexible thinking prevents your ability to see the big picture and to find creative and alternative routes toward your goal. You may shape your experience into what you think it should be by responding to present situations based on your past even when conditions have changed.

In building Resilience, it is often helpful to develop a broader perspective, keeping in mind that what you are going through is also part of a larger cycle. Despite the extremes of your immediate experience, positive or negative, events will balance themselves out over the long term.

___Keys to Managing Thoughts___: Question assumptions, attitudes and beliefs, and actively and consistently monitor and redirect your thoughts in positive directions.

A key area of importance is controlling negative thinking and replacing it with positive thinking. Negative thinking undermines Resilience because attention is focused non-productively. By reducing negative thinking, you will have a greater ability to concentrate and think clearly. Examples of negative thinking include:

- Jumping to conclusions
- Not seeing the forest for the trees, often called tunnel vision
- Personalizing, thinking everything is focused on you
- Attributing responsibility and blame to others

- Over-generalizing, applying data from one situation to an unrelated situation
- Assuming what others are thinking instead of asking

An example of controlling negative thinking is when you are criticized and jump to the conclusion that a stakeholder did not value the interactions or your expertise. You might take the criticism personally, concluding that your relationship or job is in jeopardy. An antidote to these two types of negative thinking, personalizing and jumping to conclusions, is to ask for more information. You could ask the stakeholder: "When you commented about this situation, were you including me in that statement? Is there anything you would like me do differently in our working relationship?"

How would the situation change if you automatically assumed that the person leveling the criticism was giving you valuable information to support your success and help you grow? As a leader, you can ask for feedback with a phrase such as, "Your thoughts and comments about how I am handling this are important to me and much appreciated. Do you have any suggestions about how I could improve?" The intent is to reduce defensiveness and hear support rather than criticism. And yes, there are people who really are critical and not looking out for your best interest. The goal of this exercise is to separate the few who are unsupportive from the many who are supportive.

This additional perspective and information, will give you the tools necessary to correct your thinking and behavior. If you are able to manage your thinking, you will be able to reduce the wasted energy spent on worrying and move quickly to action. This type of interaction takes discipline and practice. If you begin to assume others are trying to do the right thing and want to be successful, you will build your personal Resilience and also improve your performance.

The antidote is not always as easy as stopping a conversation and asking a clarifying question. Dealing with negative thinking is crucial because a great deal of emotional energy can be wasted on things that do not produce results and because negative thinking can have such a strong impact on Resilience, it is critical to build practices that replace negative thinking and mitigate its physiological and emotional impact. Areas to consider include building the capacity to:

- Assume best intentions even when things do not go your way
- Find ways to feel good about your role and about yourself

- Replace negative habits and activities with positive ones; also consider replacing negative people with positive people when possible, or change the dynamics of your interactions with people who may be inclined to negativity

When we facilitate workshops we spend a great deal of time on managing thinking. It is an area over which you have the greatest control because it does not require extra time or equipment like you might need to enhance an exercise program.

We worked with a CEO named Mike. When he took the leadership role, he shared his personal values card with everyone. Before taking this role, he spent a great deal of time reflecting on what he stood for as a person and as a leader. Of the ten operating guidelines he put forth, the one about assuming the best intentions from others got the greatest attention. Mike inspired amazing loyalty among his employees even during tough economic times when he needed to downsize and restructure to keep the company viable. People feel more secure about their work and themselves when working for a boss who assumes that they are working hard and doing their best. It is in an environment of safety and trust that people can engage in their work and make significant changes. This is one area most leaders have the capacity to change in a relatively short time.

Fulfill Life Purpose While Living Your Values

Having a strong sense of life purpose is a critical part of the foundation for Resilience. According to Daniel Goleman's research comparing star performers with average performers in senior leadership positions, he found that nearly ninety percent of the difference in their performance profiles was attributable to emotional intelligence factors. In leadership roles, emotional intelligence is an important factor in accomplishing life purpose. Key areas of emotional intelligence are:

- Self-awareness
- Self-management
- Social awareness
- Relationship management

The research on Emotional Intelligence (EI) as referenced in *Primal Leadership: Learning to Lead with Emotional Intelligence* by Daniel Goleman, Richard E. Boyatzis and Annie McKee suggests outstanding leaders have a high EI quotient in addition to a high IQ. Emotions impact reasoning and decision-making, and if neglected can derail your ability to implement well-structured plans. Because your emotions are contagious, your ability to manage them impacts those with whom you work. Basically, emotional intelligence addresses your ability to work with others. In leadership roles, your ability to read others and develop strong relationships allows you to accomplish your business goals.

__Keys to purpose and emotional intelligence:__ Have a clear life purpose, develop skills in self-management, and appreciate and work with your emotions regularly. We addressed part of the process of self-management when we talked about managing your negative and positive thinking. This section will focus more on developing a clear life purpose.

By understanding what you stand for, you are much better able to maintain your perspective and focus on the things you care most about. Most people find that when they know what is important to them, they have a much greater capacity to overlook the small stuff. As you clarify your purpose, you may find that things that previously bothered you begin to look like less important "small stuff." If you are not clear on your vision or purpose, we encourage you to take time to do the exercises in the chapter "Create a Compelling Vision of your Future" in either the *Innovative Leadership Fieldbook,* or in any of the innovative leadership workbooks. While most of us think we know our vision, the process of actually sitting down and writing it on paper to clarify it is a very valuable exercise.

We mentioned the CEO, Mike, earlier and the impact he had on others by sharing his operating principles. Those principles were a result of an exercise that started with his vision. Mike can tell you his vision and that clarity helps him keep a healthy perspective on the challenges he faces at work and at home. Because he knows who he is and what he stands for, his actions are consistent and people develop a high level of trust in their relationships with him.

Which opportunities in your professional life help you achieve life purpose? In addition to being clear about life purpose, it is critical to have regular activities that contribute to your ability to renew yourself. An activity that many people find helpful is meditation or prayer. Engaging in prayer can help you manage your thought process and also help you connect with something larger than yourself. Renewal contributes significantly to your ability to consistently demonstrate emotional intelligence. According to the book, *Resonant Leadership*, renewing yourself and connecting with others through mindfulness, hope, and compassion are three activities that have a significant impact on your ability to interact innovatively with others.

- **Mindfulness:** being awake, aware, and attending to the world
- **Hope:** believing that the future you envision is attainable and moving toward your vision and goals while inspiring others toward those goals as well
- **Compassion:** understanding people's wants and needs, and feeling motivated to act on those feelings

Another powerful tool to renew your emotional capacity is performing acts of kindness and service directed toward others. According to *The Economics of Well-being* by Gallup Press (2010), "When we surveyed more than 23,000 people, we found that nearly 9 in 10 report 'getting an emotional boost' from doing kind things for others…Throughout the course of our lives, 'well-doing' enhances our social interaction as well as our meaning and purpose. And some studies suggest that it inoculates us from stress and other negative emotions, thus increasing longevity."

Harness the Power of Connection

The ability to interact with awareness, empathy, and skills is vital in building Resilience. Because social awareness and relationship management are so important, we are revisiting a key factor previously mentioned in emotional intelligence. The purpose of relationship management as we are discussing it here is to use these skills to understand and work effectively with internal and external organizational stakeholders such as employees, executives, regulators, customers, and others.

According to Gallup, "Those *without a best friend* in the workplace have just a one in twelve chance of being engaged. Social relationships at work have also been shown to boost employee retention, safety, work quality and customer engagement." We use the term "relationship management" rather than "best friend" when we talk about emotional intelligence.

This Gallup research represents a significant shift in how many people view relationships at work and the importance of developing strong connections. We believe the research is clear: investing your time in connecting with colleagues improves your work and your work environment. It is equally important to maintain professionalism in business relationships and respect professional boundaries.

The belief that having strong relationships at work sustainably boosts work quality differs significantly from what many experienced early in their careers, where the prevailing attitude was to focus on tasks while at work and build relationships during personal time. You may have been actively discouraged from developing close relationships with colleagues to avoid being seen as "unprofessional." What do you believe about friendships within the work place? How do these beliefs align with the Gallup research?

A key factor in building successful relationships is communicating in a consistently open and honest manner, and doing what you say. Here are a few tips to improving your communication:

- Say things simply and clearly
- Make communication safe by being responsive
- Encourage people to ask questions and clarify if they do not understand you
- Balance advocacy for your point with inquiring about the other person's points
- When you have a different point of view, seek in a non-threatening way to understand how and why the other person believes what they do (remember, they are trying to do the right thing and be successful as well)
- When in doubt, share information and emotions
- Build trust by acting for the greater good

Keys to connection: Invest time in key relationships and build skills that are necessary in relating to others, such as communication and empathy.

Resilience and Organizational Effectiveness

Organizations benefit significantly from having resilient leaders, and yet often organizational culture and systems encourage behaviors that are at odds with Resilience. To bring about true individual and organizational change, leaders must incorporate Resilience into the larger picture of leadership development and organizational effectiveness.

As an innovative leader, you will develop action plans for transitioning your organization from the status quo to one that supports resilient leaders and workers. As an example, an innovative leader we worked with committed to encouraging employees to negotiate due dates for non-critical tasks. In this case, employees previously had not taken personal time off because they felt the need to be "on call" continually even when their tasks did not require this level of availability. Having due dates that appropriately addressed the criticality of tasks allowed them the flexibility to integrate time for exercise and better work-life balance that resulted in them feeling more energetic and engaged when on the job. By focusing on changing systems and processes, as well as promoting a culture that supports a balance of organizational results with Resilience, people within the organization will have the capacity to navigate organizational changes without being unnecessarily overwhelmed.

Application

This case study outlines an example of Resilience in action and the effect of cultivating it in the midst of professional turmoil. In this case, improvement in Resilience allowed employees to remain focused, stay engaged, and maintain productivity and safety standards while reducing the negative physical and emotional impacts of a very challenging time.

The client company consolidated production and equipment with an outside contractor and moved operations. This move offered greater scalability and featured more advanced production equipment and processes for the company and stakeholders. The company had employed 334 people, many of whom were closely related. Plant closings of this size in a rural area create hardships for workers and their families and can challenge the economic stability of the entire town.

Tom, the human resources manager, was working on his master's degree with a focus on developing hardiness and Resilience for employees and believed he would be more successful in this transition if he got additional outside help to implement a Resilience program to support this very disruptive transition. "I was looking for an organization to help facilitate the process of closing the plant and specifically [helping us address] the human resource issues that we were facing. I had a good relationship with employees and the union, and also knew that bringing in someone from outside the company had benefits," noted Tom.

Together, the plant manager, their consultants, and Tom developed a plan for employee transition and provided employee coaching during the plant closing process. The project team conducted Resilience workshops and coached company leaders during the transition. Additionally, the outside firm coached Tom on how to manage and lead the group through the changes they were about to experience.

A facilitator conducted a workshop for hourly employees, key members of management, and some union members in which Resilience during change was explored in depth. The goal was to help employees prepare for the transition and plan for their future. Employees were dealing with two different sets of challenges: staying productive while the plant was being closed, and concurrently identifying their next career steps. During the workshop and ongoing counseling, they were given tools to help them with both sets of challenges. To deal with the plant closing, they focused on topics like managing their thinking and maintaining strong connections with each other. They were encouraged to explore their own sense of purpose as they considered their next career steps. Managers were also involved in special workshops on how to plan and manage their own transition while supporting their employees and closing the plant in a professional manner.

In addition to Resilience training, the plant management team attended monthly sessions at which they discussed the challenges they were experiencing and talked about how to cope with them, and one-on-one coaching sessions for the plant management team were geared toward supporting them during this transition.

"The plant manager and I held meetings in which we acknowledged the grieving process for employees. We spent time talking and listening to individuals' experiences. In effect, we helped to mitigate the anger of the experience," explained Tom.

Table 3.2 summarizes the challenges the company faced and solutions that were provided. While these solutions were tailored to this specific organization, they can be generalized to apply to a broad range of companies.

Table 3.2

Challenge	Solution	Impact
Lack of understanding of personal Resilience	Conduct Resilience workshops to *promote awareness and use of individual Resilience tools*	Increased personal awareness and build skills
Plant leadership and departments encourage results without concern for individual Resilience impact	Department working sessions to *identify barriers to Resilience and address them systemically* while also attending to the need to deliver results	Identification and reduction (or elimination) organizational processes and beliefs that discouraged Resilience
Individuals understand what is required, but personal change is hard when focusing on business results	*Create accountability partner relationships* where individuals and groups set Resilience goals and discuss their results at regularly scheduled intervals to provide accountability and support for changing behavior	Built a culture and systems that supported resilient behavior
Leaders feeling the stress of the plant closure and personal concerns about career and family stability	Create one-on-one and group coaching opportunities tailored to address issues, build personal Resilience, and promote Resilience among broader leadership team and employees	Leaders had better skills and modeled resilient behavior encouraging employees to do the same

Results:

Using the Resilience tools discussed earlier in this chapter, "... employees were able to gain a new sense of control during the closing of their plant. As a result, accidents were reduced and the plant made every production and delivery goal, resulting in the plant making a profit for two months longer than corporate expectations and materially exceeding the capabilities of other plants that were shut down that didn't have resiliency programs," according to Tom.

This chapter provided a brief introduction of how, through building Resilience capacity, innovative leaders can increase the capacity of both individual employees and their organizations to achieve their goals. Having the ability to maintain physical well-being, manage thoughts, fulfill purpose using emotional intelligence, and harness the power of connection during times of transition is critical to successfully transforming organizations.

REFLECTION QUESTIONS

Where would you rank your Resilience in each of
the four categories?

━━━━━━━

How does increased Resilience improve your effectiveness
as a person and as a leader?

━━━━━━━

What is your biggest Resilience challenge?

━━━━━━━

Think of areas in your life where you may indulge in negative
thinking, then think of an antidote or approach to step
away from the negative thinking and replace it with positive
thinking.

━━━━━━━

How do you, as a leader, build Resilience into your
organization's systems and culture?

━━━━━━━

As a leader, how do you model resilient behavior
that is visible to others and sets the tone for your belief
that Resilience is important for your success and the
success of your people?

Resilience Quick Reference Page

This summary page provides you with a place to capture your scores, and notes about yourself and your Resilience. You can detach and use it as you read this chapter, or retain it in the book for future reference. You can take a free Resilience assessment at www.metcalf-associates.com to determine your score.

Table 3.3

Keys to Building & Retaining Personal Resilience	Your Score	Your Notes
Manage Thinking Practice telling yourself: ■ Challenges are normal and healthy for any individual or organization ■ My current problem is a doorway to an innovative solution ■ I feel inspired about the opportunity to create new possibilities that did not exist before		
Maintain Physical Well-Being Are you getting enough: ■ Sleep ■ Exercise ■ Healthy food ■ Time in nature ■ Time to meditate and relax Are you limiting or eliminating: ■ Caffeine ■ Nicotine		
Using Emotional Intelligence to Fulfill Life Purpose Understand what you stand for. Maintain focus. Ask: ■ What is my purpose? ■ Why is it important to me? ■ What values do I hold that will enable me to accomplish my purpose? ■ What opportunities in my professional life help me to achieve my life purpose?		

Keys to Building & Retaining Personal Resilience	Your Score	Your Notes
Harness the Power of Connection Practice effective communication: - Say things simply and clearly - Make communication safe by being responsive - Encourage people to ask questions and clarify if they do not understand your message - Balance advocacy for your point with inquiring about the other person's points - When you have a different point of view, seek to understand how and why the other person believes what they do in a non-threatening way - When in doubt, share information and emotions - Build trust by acting for the greater good		
TOTAL	100%	

CHAPTER 4
Situational Analysis

Fig. 4.1 Five Elements of Innovative Leadership

Leadership Behaviors

Situational Analysis

Resilience

Developmental Perspective

Leader Type

While we have focused heavily thus far on building individual capacity for leaders and employees, understanding the organization's background or context is equally important. Consider that your experience isn't merely a collection of events and random happenstance; rather, it is fundamentally shaped by the background interplay of your individual attributes, shared relationships, and involved institutions. In other words, experiences not only unfold as expressions of your unique personal views, but are also culturally filtered through your interpersonal relationships with others, objectively affected in your behaviors, and socially distributed through your networks and technological systems.

The Importance of Situational Analysis

The nature of human experience is more than simple personal expression. Every moment of experience is influenced by a mutual interaction of intention (self), action, culture, and systems. All four of these basic dimensions are fundamental to every experience we have and mutually shape them in all circumstances. Situational Analysis involves employing the four-dimensional view of reality Figure 4.2 to balance in the most comprehensive way possible the situations you face. This balance of qualities—without favoring elements—is critical to effectively transform your organization.

A multi-faceted approach provides a more complete and accurate view of events and situations than the traditional approach that often favors analysis based primarily on a systems or process view and excludes culture and leadership impact. Leaders often take a partial approach to changing organizations. They overemphasize systems change with little or no consideration to the culture or how their personal views and actions shape the content and success of the change. Situational Analysis enables you to create alignment across the four dimensions on an ongoing basis.

Integral Model and Situational Awareness

Fig. 4.2 Integral Model

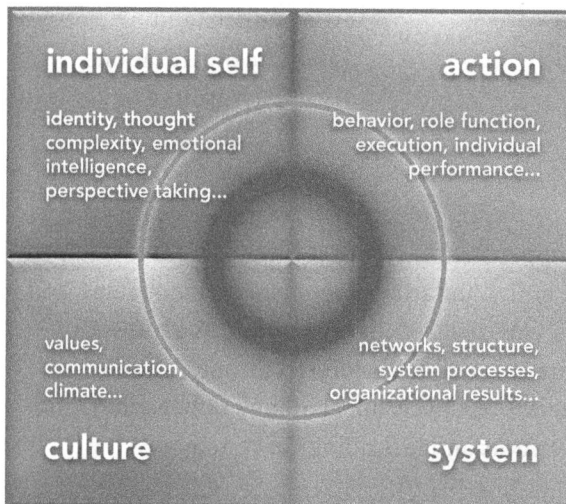

individual self	action
identity, thought complexity, emotional intelligence, perspective taking...	behavior, role function, execution, individual performance...
values, communication, climate...	networks, structure, system processes, organizational results...
culture	system

American-born philosopher Ken Wilber developed a conceptual scheme to illustrate the four basic dimensions of being that form the backbone of experience. His Integral Model provides a map that shows the mutual relationship and interconnection among four dimensions in which each represents the basic elements of human experience.

When using Situational Analysis, you are cultivating simultaneous awareness of all four dimensions. Let's look at an example. This is a sample narrative taken from *Integral Life Practice* (Wilber et al) that will give you a more experiential description of how these dimensions shape every situation in your life.

Example: *"Imagine yourself announcing a project that will change the organization structure ..."*

Intention (*Upper-Left Quadrant, "I"*): You feel excited and a little nervous about the big meeting today. Thoughts race through your head about how best to make the announcement knowing that some people will be concerned and anxious about changes.

Culture *(Lower-Left Quadrant, "We")*: You enter a familiar office culture of shared beliefs about what we do and shared expectations about how we accomplish our work. We have a common language to communicate and norms about what is accepted and what is not.

Action *(Upper-Right, "It")*: Your physical behaviors are aligned with your values and those of the culture: walking into the meeting, greeting people with a friendly tone, clarifying the agenda for the meeting, making the announcement, entertaining clarifying questions. Brain activity, heart rate, and perspiration all increase as you make the announcement and sense the reaction of people in the room.

System *(Lower-Right, "Its")*: You enter a familiar well-lit office and conference room with a large meeting table and matching chairs. Mission and vision statements are framed and hanging on the walls. Some offices also have framed photos of the founder. People enter the meeting room a couple of minutes early, and the meeting follows standard meeting process, kicked off by the leader who states the purpose and agenda.

A crucial part of transforming your organization is leveraging your capacity as an innovative leader to be aware of the four dimensions at any given moment and to identify alignments and misalignments. Even though you cannot physically see the values, beliefs, and emotions that strongly influence the way an individual colleague perceives himself and the world, nor a group's culture, emotional climate or collective perception, they still profoundly shape the vision and potential of leaders to address adaptive problems and transform an organization.

Alignment and Influence

We use an alignment model to describe how using Situational Analysis as a tool allows you not only to make more informed decisions, but also helps you optimize performance within yourself, your teams, and the broader organization. Alignment of all dimensions is the key to optimizing performance.

Alignment across the four dimensions starts with self, culture, action and systems, and explores how these dimensions create an aligned system that is cohesive and integrated. Figure 4-3 shows the image of an aligned system and the following section describes how the dimensions are aligned.

Fig. 4.3 Alignments across Dimensions

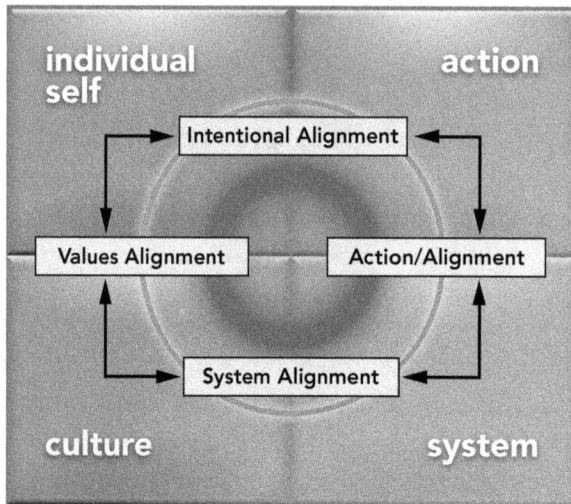

- **Personal Alignment:** The ongoing process of coordinating your self-dimension (intentions, identify, thoughts, emotional intelligence, and perspective taking) with your action dimension (behavior, role function, execution, individual performance) to create a sense of personal integrity within yourself and inspire trust in others.

- **Action Alignment:** The ongoing process of coordinating your action-dimension (behavior, role function, execution, individual performance) with the organization's system-dimension (network, structure, system processes, and organizational results) to create recognition for yourself and efficient and effective organizational results.

- **System Alignment:** The ongoing process of coordinating system-dimension (network, structure, system processes, and organizational results) with the culture-dimension (organizational values, communication and climate) to increase functional efficiency among organizational culture and systems.

- **Values Alignment:** The ongoing process of coordinating the culture-dimension (organizational values, communication, and climate) with the self-dimension (intentions, identify, thoughts, emotional intelligence, and perspective taking) to create a sense of individual alignment with organizational values that cause individuals to feel they "fit" in the organization and that the organization has a sense of value-based leaders.

While we have not drawn the arrows on the diagonal, when the dimensions are aligned as shown in Figure 4.3, all dimensions reflect balance. This alignment is important because it minimizes confusion and productivity loss. When misaligned, employees are often given conflicting direction or told to act in one way then penalized during the appraisal process because different behaviors are rewarded rather than behaviors they were told to change.

Application

Following is an example where a project manager used the Situational Analysis model during the implementation of an enterprise-wide employee recognition system that impacted 30,000 workers. The project focused on assessing options and selecting and implementing a solution that would improve employee engagement. The project manager considered all dimensions to ensure that the solution chosen was as comprehensive as possible, and successfully implemented the system to create long-term impact on employee engagement, client retention, and satisfaction. The project manager worked with an implementation team consisting of client employees and members from the team that sold the recognition system.

- **Personal Alignment:** In agreeing to take on the project, the project manager evaluated commitment to this assignment by checking personal values against the actions that would be required for implementation. The project manager was personally committed to employee recognition as a tool to increase associate engagement while positively impacting customer enthusiasm and business results. The project was well-aligned with the project manager's personal belief about how companies recognize employees in ways that are personally meaningful, and linking performance to organizational strategy, culture, and systems. This project was designed to accomplish all of these outcomes. The project manager could take the actions required to perform the role and maintain alignment between self and action. Had the project been inconsistent with the leader's values, it may have been difficult for her to promote projects that she either did not believe in, or is personally offended by. She may still have chosen to go forward, but this misalignment would impact her engagement and possibly her success.

- **Action Alignment:** The project manager continually verified that she and the actions of the implementation team were aligned with the organizational systems. Additionally, she verified that all participants were in roles for which they were well qualified. She worked within the established systems and structures of the organization. Understanding and working within the prevailing systems allowed the implementation team to function effectively with minimal disruption to the existing structure. If the team was creating something novel, it may have needed to give more effort to determine where the existing systems would not support the change and where it might create new processes or systems and need to align these with the rest of the organization.

- **System Alignment:** The system here is defined as the performance management systems and processes within the organization, as well as the new recognition system. The project manager evaluated how the recognition system would align to the existing performance management systems and company culture, as well as the team selecting options with similar alignment. A key part of the implementation process was tailoring the recognition system to fit the culture and align with the multiple existing performance management systems. One way the recognition system reflected the culture was to create an option to recognize employees for living the company values. By the time the recognition system was launched, it was closely aligned with the company culture and integrated into the existing performance management systems.

  There was an element of the system that needed to be addressed. When receiving monetary recognition, even if just a twenty-five dollar gift card, the employee's pay check was adjusted for taxes on that reward. The organization needed to determine its policy about augmenting bonuses and awards to account for taxes. While on the surface this seems like a very simple question, the team needed to consider a range of situations from how executives are compensated to how hourly employees are compensated. The policy for the reward system took into account the organizational values about fairness and the culture of equity. The system was then configured to address the tax consequences of rewards.

- **Values Alignment:** In this project, the culture was defined as the culture of the organization implementing the reward system. The project manager evaluated the connection between self-dimension and company values. As mentioned in action alignment, the project manager valued employee recognition. The company expressly stated they valued people, honesty and integrity, coaching and feedback, and several others. The project manager's values were aligned with the company values, allowing the project manager to act with a sense of integrity in that the client would not ask her to do anything that conflicted with her values.

The project manager was aware of the four dimensions concurrently and paid attention to the impact created during the initial alignment. By giving balanced attention to all dimensions and ensuring alignment, the project manager led the team to successfully complete a project that ensured an immediate and long-term impact on the organization. Because she considered the interplay between all four dimensions, she was able to work with the team to identify solutions to issues that could have derailed the project success. The project received positive feedback after its launch because of the ease and success of the release. Additionally, it is being used extensively by employees, with over 15,000 recognition messages sent within the first six months.

Increased Situational Analysis helps you create holistic solutions by removing misalignment among the four key dimensions. The process of deliberately evaluating the four basic dimensions of any experience can provide you with a tool to identify potential disconnects that could waste resources and cause great frustration for you and your employees. From a leadership perspective Situational Analysis will allow you to have greater impact because you have taken the deliberate step to align all the dimensions.

This chapter has provided a brief introduction to Situational Analysis and the integral model. The goal of Situational Analysis is to align the four dimensions through deliberate understanding of the dimensions and the interconnections across each one. Deliberately focusing on alignment is a key lever to implementing innovative changes that allow your organization to thrive.

REFLECTION QUESTIONS

Do you work for an organization that is aligned with your personal purpose and values?

▰▰▰▰▰▰▰

How often do you take time to consider how you think or feel about a task before you move forward?

▰▰▰▰▰▰▰

Where do you see misalignment between what you value and how you act because of pressure from your organization?

▰▰▰▰▰▰▰

Where do you see misalignment between what your organization says it values and the systems it has put in place, such as performance management and compensation?

▰▰▰▰▰▰▰

As you are implementing change, how will you use Situational Analysis to ensure that all dimensions are addressed and aligned?

▰▰▰▰▰▰▰

How will you use your understanding of Situational Analysis to make important decisions, considering the alignment of all four dimensions and the impact each has on the successful outcome?

CHAPTER 5
Leadership Behaviors

Fig. 5.1 Five Elements of Innovative Leadership

Leadership Behaviors

Situational Analysis

Resilience

Developmental Perspective

Leader Type

In previous chapters we explored how understanding type and Developmental Perspective will enhance your ability to transform your organization. Next we discussed why Resilience is important to building the capacity of those implementing the transformation as well as those who are affected and whose jobs are being transformed. We further examined the four dimensions of experience and how Situational Analysis can promote alignment across the dimensions to increase efficiency and effectiveness along with a sense of personal integrity. Now it is time to explore the fifth and final dimension of innovative leadership: Leadership Behaviors.

The Importance of Leadership Behaviors

As we shift our focus to the more actionable craft of leadership as defined by behaviors and skills, we will examine the impact of observable leadership skills for the leader and the leadership team. Leadership skills as well as hard skills are critical to success and serve as objective performance measures of innovative leadership. Hard skills fall into two primary categories: industry-related knowledge, skills, and aptitudes; and functional knowledge, skills, and aptitudes. Leadership Behaviors are the result of knowledge, skills, and aptitudes specifically related to the craft of leadership. We will be using the term Leadership Behaviors in this guide when referring to leadership knowledge, skills and aptitudes and the resulting behaviors. Both hard skills and Leadership Behaviors are critical to successful organizational transformation. The balance between the importance of hard skills and Leadership Behaviors will shift as the leader progresses in the organization and as leadership skills and behaviors become increasingly important with career advancement and complex roles involving the implementation of organizational transformation.

Leadership Behaviors are important because they *are the objective actions the leader takes that transform the organization and impact organizational success.* We have all seen brilliant leaders behave in a manner that damages their organization and we have seen other leaders consistently behave in ways that promote ongoing organizational success. Effective leadership behavior drives organizational success and, conversely, ineffective leadership behaviors drive organizational dysfunction or failure. In this chapter we will look at the Leadership Behaviors associated with innovative leadership and successful organizational transformation for both individual leaders and leadership teams.

An example of the need for both hard skills and Leadership Behaviors is in the role as a hospital CEO. To be successful, this CEO must possess the hard skills in hospital administration to understand how the hospital operates and the Leadership Behaviors to effectively lead. If either of these sets of skills is missing, the leader and the hospital are at risk of failure. Early in his career, a mastery of hospital administration set him apart from his peers. As he progressed into the senior leadership ranks and ultimately to the role of CEO, his use of Leadership Behaviors became his primary focus while he continued to also need hard skills and expertise in hospital administration.

One area we have not yet discussed is that of making decisions about who is on the leadership team and who is not. These decisions involve promotions and move people into new roles and possibly out of the company. The following section is about leadership behaviors from a self-development perspective. As a leader, which behaviors support the organization's success, and which ones do not? It is important to gauge the balance between development and performance management. One of the quickest ways to kill development is to tell staff you want them to participate in development activities and then begin firing people—particularly those who have scored low. We acknowledge that performance management is critical to organizational success—it must be aligned as we need to develop the characteristics to successfully run an organization. That said, we need to send clear messages about creating a safety zone in which people can develop—especially top performers who are consistently improving themselves and rising stars who still have plenty of growing to do. Later in the book we'll talk about who is involved in key projects and in which roles.

You may notice that many of our examples are drawn from larger companies. While we believe these activities are important for companies of all sizes, our experiences are often with larger organizations that retain us for our services. We also use these tools in our companies, some large and some small. These tools may actually be more important in small companies as the margin for error often is less. While mistakes impact companies of all sizes, smaller companies are affected to a greater extent and many go out of business when mistakes are made.

The Leadership Circle Profile™ and Leadership Behaviors

There are several different ways to discuss leadership from a skills perspective as demonstrated by Peter G. Northouse in his book, *Leadership Theory and Practice:*

> *There are several strengths in conceptualizing leadership from a skills [actions] perspective. First, it is a leader-centered model that stresses the importance of the leader's abilities, and it places learning skills at the center of effective leadership performance. Second, the skills approach describes leadership in such a way that it makes it available to everyone. Skills are behaviors that we all can learn to develop and improve. Third, the skills approach provides a sophisticated map that explains how effective leadership performance can be achieved.*

We will use an assessment model to discuss leadership behaviors just as we used the Enneagram to measure personality type and the MAP to measure Developmental Perspective level. We use the **Leadership Circle Profile** (LCP) and the associated framework from the Leadership Circle® to explore Leadership Behaviors.

The LCP is an assessment tool that collects feedback from the leader's boss, boss's boss, peers, and subordinates to provide a 360-degree perspective of the leader's performance along with the leader's self-assessment. The most effective leadership behavior assessments are solidly researched and measure behaviors shown to correlate to leadership effectiveness and to key business outcomes. The LCP is a powerful competency-based assessment that includes the belief systems and assumptions underpinning a leader's behavior. This tool integrates well with other tools such as the Enneagram and MAP in a way that provides great insight to leaders.

The results can also be aggregated to measure a leadership team and the leadership culture. These measures can be very helpful when implementing significant organizational change as they help determine how they perform as a team compared to the performance of each individual. The aggregate score also gives a great deal of insight into the leadership culture and, as a team, they can determine if the current team score supports the change they are trying to make. This tool also helps them identify gaps between personal views of performance versus how others see them. Because it is critical for leaders to "walk the talk," having a tool that helps leaders increase their self-awareness is very helpful.

Although the LCP incorporates elements of type, beliefs, and Developmental Perspective, we are positioning it in this guide to address individual and team leadership behaviors as well as leadership culture. The purpose of going into detail here is to give insight into the actual behaviors associated with innovative leaders and successful organizational transformation.

As the reader using this guide, you may choose to use the assessments we have discussed (Enneagram, MAP, and LCP), or others. We recommend the suite of tools we have discussed because they work well together and in many cases the theories underpinning the assessments are also aligned. If you select other tools, we recommend you research the interconnections or conflicts that may arise from the information provided.

As with the discussion on the Enneagram assessment, it is critical to use an assessment tool effectively to receive the benefit from it. Unlike the Enneagram, many leaders do not share their individual LCP scores with teammates. The LCP is designed to provide detailed information to the leader to support individual and team development. For many leaders these results show weaknesses that they would like to keep private—yet we encourage you as a leader to select a trusted colleague to provide you with ongoing support and feedback to meet your development goals. This will likely mean you share your scores with another team member. If the organization is using a 360-assessment across the leadership team, it will be important to set expectations in advance to define who will see the data and how it will be used. It should be positioned in a way that supports participants answering honestly and leaders using the resulting scores to improve their performance as well as overall team success.

The Leadership Circle Profile (LCP) Behaviors

Fig. 5.2 Leadership Circle Profile

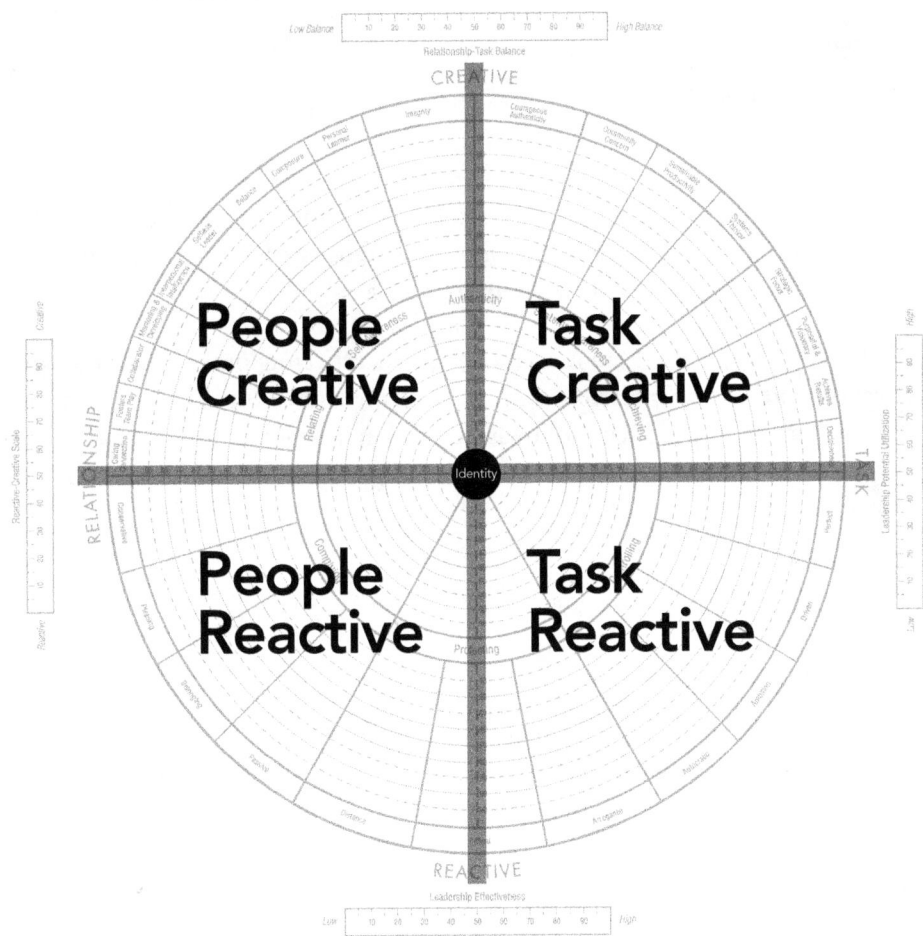

The Leadership Circle measures key dimensions of leadership shown in the inner circle in Figure 5.2. The sub-categories are then shown in the outer circle. These are broken into four key dimensions: people creative, task creative, people reactive, and task reactive. These four categories are created by drawing a line through the circle horizontally to separate the creative and reactive dimensions. The second line is drawn vertically to separate people and task dimensions.

The top of the circle behaviors are ***creative behaviors***:

- Relating
- Self-awareness
- Authenticity
- Systems Awareness
- Achieving

These behaviors reflect proactive action, referred to by the Leadership Circle as "Creative." ***These behaviors reflect behaviors associated with setting strategic direction and inspiring people to accomplish goals.***

The bottom half of the circle are ***reactive behaviors reflecting inner beliefs that limit effectiveness, authentic expression, and empowering leadership.*** These dimensions reflect behaviors associated with following direction or reacting to circumstances as they arise rather than setting direction and creating the conditions for success. These behaviors include:

- Controlling
- Protecting
- Complying

The creative and reactive dimensions are then split on the vertical axis between people and task behaviors. People behaviors are associated with the actions leaders take to build themselves and their people, such as self-awareness and relating better with others. The task behaviors are actions leaders take associated with the work of running a business, such as systems awareness and achieving.

The blend of the four LCP dimensions required to be innovative will depend on the situation and organization. It is important to understand the behaviors associated with innovative leadership and also to be able to flex your own leadership behaviors to match what is required by the organization. The most effective leaders and organizations demonstrate behaviors heavily weighted on the creative end of the scale. The balance between task and relationship will depend in part on the role of the leader within the organization. Strong leaders have the capacity to perform both people- and task-related roles well.

According to the *Leadership Circle Participant Profile Manual,* 2009 edition, published by the Leadership Circle, "These competencies [behaviors] have been well researched and shown to be the most critical behaviors and skill sets for leaders."

Table 5.1

LCP DIMENSION DEFINITIONS

The Creative Leadership Behaviors reflect key behaviors and internal assumptions that lead to <u>high fulfillment, high achievement leadership</u>.

The **Relating** Dimension measures a leader's capability to relate to others in a way that brings out the best in people, groups, and organizations. It comprises:

- Caring Connection
- Fosters Team Play
- Collaborator
- Mentoring and Developing
- Interpersonal Intelligence

The **Self-Awareness** Dimension measures the leader's orientation to ongoing professional and personal development, as well as the degree to which inner self-awareness is expressed through high integrity leadership. It comprises:

- Selfless Leader
- Balance
- Composure
- Personal Learner

The **Authenticity** Dimension measures the leader's capability to relate to others with high integrity in an authentic and courageous manner. It comprises:

- Integrity
- Authenticity

The **Systems Awareness** Dimension measures the degree to which the leader's awareness is focused on whole system improvement and on community welfare (the symbiotic relationship between the long-term welfare of the community and the interests of the organization). It comprises:

- Community Concern
- Sustainable Productivity
- Systems Thinker

The **Achieving** Dimension measures the extent to which the leader offers visionary, authentic, and high accomplishment leadership. It comprises:

- Strategic Focus
- Purposeful and Visionary
- Achieves Results
- Decisiveness

The *Reactive Leadership Styles* reflect inner beliefs that limit effectiveness, authentic expression, and empowering leadership.

The **Controlling** Dimension measures the extent to which the leader establishes a sense of personal worth through task accomplishment and personal achievement. Dimensions include: ▪ Perfect ▪ Driven ▪ Ambition ▪ Autocratic	The **Protecting** Dimension which measures the belief that the leader can feel safe and establish a sense of worth through withdrawal, remaining distant, hidden, aloof, cynical, superior, and/or rational. Dimensions include: ▪ Arrogance ▪ Critical ▪ Distance
The **Complying** Dimension measures the extent to which the leader gets a sense of self-worth and security by following the direction of others rather than acting on his own intentions and wants. Dimensions include: ▪ Conservative ▪ Pleasing ▪ Belonging ▪ Passive	

Leadership Behaviors and Organizational Effectiveness

Effective leadership behaviors drive effective organizations. As we build on the Situational Analysis model, effective leaders' behaviors, also referred to as "actions" in the Situational Analysis model, are one of the four dimensions (upper right quadrant). If these behaviors or actions are aligned with the other dimensions, then the whole system is affected by who the leader is and how the leader behaves. According to the alignment component of the Situational Analysis model, effective leaders align self and actions to create personal alignment; they align self and cultures to create values alignment; they align their actions and systems to create action alignment; and they align cultures and systems to create system alignment. If the leader's behaviors or actions are ineffective, the entire system will be ineffective. If their behaviors are ineffective and the system is not aligned, they will still cause organizational dysfunction. If, on the other hand, the leader is behaving in a manner that supports the organization and creates alignment across the dimensions, the entire organization will benefit. The behaviors in the LCP that are most effective are those represented by the creative dimensions: relating, self-awareness, authenticity, systems awareness, and achieving.

Application – Case Study

A global manufacturing company hired a new CIO in the middle of a complex organization-wide change project that included a significant technology component. The new CIO hired a consultant to work with him as he took the new role. The firm provided coaching and consulting support including:

- Facilitating organizational planning sessions
- Identifying the strengths and weaknesses of leaders
- Coaching leaders to increase individual effectiveness
- Identifying strengths and weaknesses of the leadership team
- Improving leadership team effectiveness
- Identifying culture and guiding principles associated with the organizational success to support organizational restructuring
- Facilitating IT organization change planning and implementation

As part of the individual and team leadership effectiveness assessment, the consultant administered the LCP assessment and found that the leaders worked in a way that would be considered primarily reactive. The new CIO recognized the risk the leadership team behavior posed to its ability to successfully implement the organization-wide change in which they were involved. The consultant used the results of the LCP assessment as the foundation for the leadership change process that supported the overall organizational change process.

One of the first steps in the development process was assessment scoring and feedback followed by education. At the same time the leaders were getting assessed, they were also looking at the guiding principles and culture they needed to successfully accomplish their goals. The leaders identified how they needed to change themselves, how they needed to change the culture and guiding principles, and how they needed to change the evaluation system that supported the old behaviors. The leaders worked with the CIO to revise the IT Department leadership performance evaluation process to formally appraise leadership behaviors along with results.

This project changed all four dimensions (leader intentions, behaviors, culture, and systems) to ensure that they could successfully lead the larger organizational transformation. In this case, they took on a small IT change process in the context of the overall organization-wide project to ensure that they could successfully meet their objectives.

To focus on the leadership behavior portion of the project, each leader took the LCP. The consultant consolidated the individual leader scores into a team score to allow the CIO to see the overall leadership team behaviors. The composite chart showed:

- The group scored high on the reactive behaviors—such as passive and belonging—associated in the complying dimension. These scores indicated challenges with accomplishing creative results, as they are associated with leaders who wait to be told what to do. This data helped the CIO to identify some key behaviors that put his ability at risk to accomplish his goals. Some of the behaviors were attributed to the leaders themselves and some of the behaviors were a product of the culture his predecessors had created.

- The group scored low in many of the creative dimensions that are important to success, such as "achieves results." This data gave the individual leaders important information for improving their effectiveness. It also provided data to the overall leadership group and the CIO about how the leaders worked together and where their behaviors needed to improve.

The organization benefitted from this process through:

- ***Increased self-awareness of individual leaders drove behavioral change.*** Each leader was able to see how he or she was perceived by others: boss, boss's boss, peers, and subordinates. The 360 part of the assessment was very helpful in giving each leader a clear and quantifiable picture of possible issues identified by others. For many leaders, there were significant surprises. These surprises became very important as the leaders learned about potential pitfalls and areas where they excelled. The consultant met with each leader and created a leadership improvement plan that focused specifically on behavioral changes. The consultant then met on a regular basis with each leader to support his development. As an example: One leader scored one (on a score of 1 to 100) on Achieves Results. He came to understand that while he perceived himself as a high performer, his peers did not. This data was an important wake-up call that he needed to make changes and make them quickly.

- ■ *Increased awareness of individual dynamics within the group.* Because the consultant consolidated the team scores, each individual was able to identify areas where his or her style differed from that of the team. In some areas, these differences explained strains in relationships people had with one another. Each individual was able to evaluate his or her fit within the team. Where areas of concern appeared, the coach added the required behavioral changes to the leader's behavioral change plan.

- ■ *Increased awareness of group dynamics.* The leadership team looked at the collective scores and determined what they liked about how they operated as a group and what they would like to change about the dynamics within the group. The consultant facilitated a leadership team-building process to define new behaviors and rules of engagement that supported increased team effectiveness and the creation of a better working environment. As the team identified how they wanted to work going forward, these changes were translated back into individual development goals for each leader given his or her unique behavioral profile.

While the initial LCP scores were low—in the bottom twenty-five percent—in some key areas, the organization was able to make significant changes over the short-term and retain some of them over the long-term. The use of the Leadership Circle Assessment tool was very important to the new CIO because it gave him important information about key areas of strength and also areas of development that posed immediate risk among his leaders. The assessment results allowed him to quickly address the most immediate gaps and opportunities, and then develop a systematic plan to make longer-term changes. It also helped him identify and leverage the leaders with the greatest strengths.

This assessment tool also gave the leaders key information. As the CIO talked about the types of behaviors he expected going forward, some of the leaders on his team determined that they did not fit in the organization going forward. Some took different roles and some left the organization. The increased self-awareness referenced above helped some of the leaders identify their own gaps and the type of working environment they preferred going forward. Some were not aligned with the changes being made and, while they had been strong performers in the past, were not aligned with the CIOs vision and approach. It is important to note that open discussions of change in leadership behaviors and norms often result in leaders choosing to leave their role rather than adapt. While these changes can be very challenging in the short term, they are often foundational to the overall organizational success. When taking on major change initiatives, the leadership team must work in alignment for the same goals and use consistent approaches to team and project leadership.

This chapter has provided a brief introduction to how Leadership Behaviors fit within the overall innovative leadership framework. Leadership Behaviors are objective and measurable actions. Understanding the behaviors associated with innovative leadership, as reflected in the LCP, creates the foundation for you to examine your own behavior and determine where you are functioning as an innovative leader and where you would like to make changes. It also supports you in aggregating individual scores to develop a team profile, understanding your greatest strengths and risks. This increased understanding can help you not only identify areas of improvement, but can also leverage the strengths you already have across the team that may not have been fully visible prior to the assessment.

REFLECTION QUESTIONS

If you were to receive feedback on your leadership competencies, where would you excel? Where would you fall short?

■■■■■■■

What percentage of your behavior would an outside observer rank as creative? Reactive?

■■■■■■■

Do you prefer task-focused activities? Relationship-focused activities? What is the percentage split you would assign to each?

■■■■■■■

Does your leadership behavioral preference match the requirements of your job?

■■■■■■■

How do you use your understanding of leadership behaviors to increase your team effectiveness?

■■■■■■■

Does your leadership team have any blind spots where they rank themselves significantly differently than where others rank them?

Leadership Behaviors Quick Reference

This summary page provides you with a place to capture your estimates of your scores, and notes about yourself and your Leadership Behaviors. You can detach and use it as you read this chapter, or retain it in the book for future reference.

As with Developmental Perspective, we do not have a recommended free or low cost assessment. As we discussed in the Situational Analysis chapter, highly effective leaders adjust their behaviors to the organization's requirements. As you will see in the assessment chapter, we recommend this as not only an individual leadership assessment, but also as a highly effective tool when evaluating teams for behaviors and culture. Please use this section to note how your situation impacts the leadership decisions.

Table 5.2

LCP Dimension Definitions	Your Notes
The Creative Leadership Behaviors reflect key behaviors and internal assumptions that lead to <u>high fulfillment, high achievement leadership</u>.	
The **Relating** Dimension measures a leader's capability to relate to others in a way that brings out the best in people, groups and organizations. It comprises: ■ Caring Connection ■ Fosters Team Play ■ Collaborator ■ Mentoring and Developing ■ Interpersonal Intelligence	
The **Self-Awareness** Dimension measures the leader's orientation to ongoing professional and personal development, as well as the degree to which inner self-awareness is expressed through high integrity leadership. It comprises: ■ Selfless Leader ■ Balance ■ Composure ■ Personal Learner	

The **Authenticity** Dimension measures the leader's capability to relate to others in an authentic, courageous, and high integrity manner. It comprises:	
■ Integrity	
■ Authenticity	
The **Systems Awareness** Dimension measures the degree to which the leader's awareness is focused on whole system improvement and on community welfare (the symbiotic relationship between the long-term welfare of the community and the interests of the organization). It comprises:	
■ Community Concern	
■ Sustainable Productivity	
■ Systems Thinker	
The **Achieving** Dimension measures the extent to which the leader offers visionary, authentic, and high accomplishment leadership. It comprises:	
■ Strategic Focus	
■ Purposeful and Visionary	
■ Achieves Results	
■ Decisiveness	

The *Reactive Leadership Styles* reflect inner beliefs that <u>limit effectiveness, authentic expression, and empowering leadership</u>.

The **Controlling** Dimension measures the extent to which the leader establishes a sense of personal worth through task accomplishment and personal achievement. Dimensions include:	
■ Perfect	
■ Driven	
■ Ambition	
■ Autocratic	

LCP Dimension Definitions	Your Score	Your Notes
The **Protecting** Dimension which measures the belief that the leader can feel safe and establish a sense of worth through withdrawal, remaining distant, hidden, aloof, cynical, superior, and/or rational. Dimensions include: ■ Arrogance ■ Critical ■ Distance		
The **Complying** Dimension measures the extent to which the leader gets a sense of self-worth and security by following the direction of others rather than acting on his own intentions and wants. Dimensions include: ■ Conservative ■ Pleasing ■ Belonging ■ Passive		
TOTAL	100%	

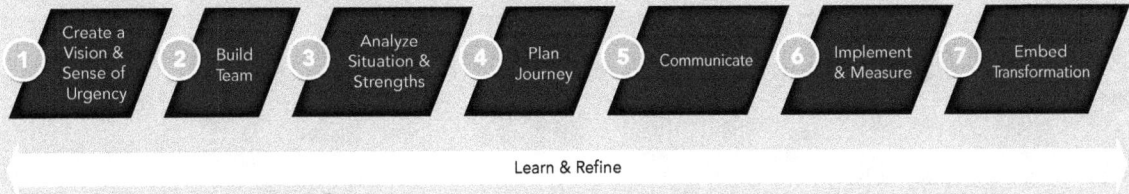

Create a Vision & Sense of Urgency — 1 · Build Team — 2 · Analyze Situation & Strengths — 3 · Plan Journey — 4 · Communicate — 5 · Implement & Measure — 6 · Embed Transformation — 7

Learn & Refine

SECTION II
The Art of Transformation

In Section I we defined and explained the five key elements of innovative leadership used by leaders and leadership teams to create a foundation for implementing organizational transformation. Using *The Art of Leading Organizational Transformation*, this interactive section of the guide contains exercises, worksheets, reflection questions, and examples, and is designed to provide a step-by-step process to support you in successfully leading your organizational transformation.

This guide has been tested with clients, as well as hundreds of working adults participating in an MBA program. It has been tested and revised over twelve years to create a process that makes a high impact on leader's capacity to transform organizations. The process steps are:

- Create a vision and sense of urgency
- Recruiting and building team
- Analyze situation and strengths
- Plan journey
- Communicate
- Implement and measure
- Embed transformation

The comprehensiveness of these exercises coupled with reflection exercises will give you the necessary insight into yourself and your organization to lead your organizational transformation. While this process appears linear, we have found that when leaders work through these steps they often return to earlier stages of the process to clarify and sometimes change details they had originally thought were correct. The structure of our process will continue to challenge you to refine the work you have accomplished in prior tasks. First ideas are often good ones, but when you work through the process and build on your knowledge, you will often find you will benefit from returning to earlier steps and refining your information.

The time you spend working on the guide is an investment in your development and your organization's transformation success. Leading a transformation effort requires reflection and thorough evaluation of both yourself and the organization. This reflection will take time and is critical to your success. We strongly encourage you to engage in the process with as much time and attention as possible. The value you ultimately take from this process is closely linked to the time you invest.

CHAPTER 6
Create a Vision and Sense of Urgency

Fig. 6.1 Innovative Leadership Development Process

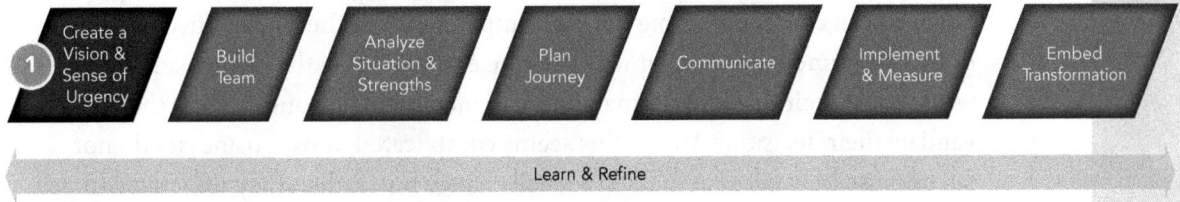

| 1 Create a Vision & Sense of Urgency | Build Team | Analyze Situation & Strengths | Plan Journey | Communicate | Implement & Measure | Embed Transformation |

Learn & Refine

The first stage of successful large-scale transformation is to ensure that key stakeholders understand the vision of the transformation, the guiding principles, and why the change is urgent and necessary. Along with defining the reason for the project, it is important for the leaders who are chartering the project to clearly convey what they expect the organization to accomplish, who will accomplish it, and how success will be measured.

This project vision and sense of urgency generally begin at the top of the organization or business unit with those who charter or authorize the change. They must be aligned with the overall organizational vision and guiding principles (or the principles that the organization is moving toward) and move the organization toward accomplishing strategic objectives.

While leaders charter the change, often employees have known for some time that a change is needed, and many are willing and able to participate and champion the movement from inside the organization. Many of these supportive employees will volunteer to work on the project in varying capacities.

The outcomes of this phase are that leaders and key stakeholders have a clear understanding of the foundation for the change that aligns the project with the overall organizational strategy, and a project charter that empowers a specific set of leaders and employees to embark on the change project.

Tools

The first task is to decide what should be transformed to help the organization to meet its strategic objectives. The leadership team clarifies the vision, goals, and business value for the change. During this process they also look at the cost involved by *not* implementing the project. Because leading a transformational change in a business can constitute a "big bet," it is imperative that the leaders involved have both a clear understanding of why they are embarking on the change and look at ways to test their thinking by making small incremental changes along the way to validate their decisions. While this seems complicated, most businesses do not fail because they failed at making a small change but, rather, they wagered and discovered that either the bet was wrong or the business environment changed along the way and the direction they were taking was no longer the one they should have taken. For these reasons, it is important to look at how to manage the risk associated with organizational transformation. For a project like we will see in the case study, the steering committee decided to implement in phases and one site at a time. We will read more about those decisions in the case study. In many cases you will find organizations using agile processes to speed up and get more value out of IT projects. Agile processes are based on iterative and incremental development methodologies.

One of the tools we like to use to help determine which project to take on to meet the strategic goals is the Change Foundation Assessment. It is likely that you, as part of the leadership team, will evaluate many potential change projects using several of these assessments, and the organization will rank the various projects and determine which ones to take on and how they are time-phased to provide the greatest benefit at the least cost and disruption to the organization.

Change Foundation Assessment

Objective: The foundation assessment is designed to help you understand and clearly articulate why the project is happening and serves as the basis for next steps in data collection. In addition, the analysis begins to build the foundation for the charter and the information that will be communicated in the awareness packages to new project team members and change network (people who support the project on a part-time or ad-hoc basis). As you explore which possible changes will help you accomplish your vision, it will be important to revisit the idea of adaptive challenges (presented in the introduction), remembering that they require concurrent changes to all four dimensions of the system, the leader's intentions and behaviors, along with the organization's culture and systems. It will be important to take this into account when defining the change and the change foundation.

Table 6.1

Change Foundation Assessment – Key Components
Data source: May include latest company strategy documents/presentations, research reports, management meeting presentation slides, white papers, etc.
Organizational vision: The organization's fundamental, enduring reason for being. A clear articulation of why the organization exists
Strategic goal: Which part of the organizational strategy does this project support?
Project objectives: Describe what the project will accomplish, or the business value it will deliver, and how success will be measured
Key stakeholders: Describe key stakeholders' understanding of the change initiative's objectives and how they fully support the organizational change required/sought
Diagnostic activities: Which analysis has been used to evaluate the project and confirm the situation?
Expected changes: Aspects of the present state that will have to change
Approval: Who authorized the project?
Project motivation: What is the motivation to pursue a different state from what it is currently?
Implementation activities: What are the high level activities required for successful implementation?
Processes in scope: What processes will be impacted by the change?
Resources: Considerations should include sufficient and available work force, budget, competencies to ensure successful transformation

Risk management: How can the project be broken into phases to manage investment and risk?

Sponsors: Who are the individuals or groups with the power to sanction or legitimize change?

Measurable outcomes: What specific changes or results will the organization use to evaluate project success?

After projects have been evaluated and a project—or more likely a series of projects—is selected for implementation, it is time to create a project charter for each project.

Project Charter

Objective: Formal document is designed to establish the project and clarify project goals (what is expected) at a high level and how it will be accomplished (guiding principles, assumptions and constraints). The charter will include information you identify in the reflection questions below.

You'll find that you have already gathered much of the information in the assessment phase you need for your charter. You'll take the information from the projects determined to have met the requirements as full scale projects and add the additional information needed to charter a team. You may find you enhance the information from the assessment phase depending on your specific situation and approach.

Creating the charter overlaps with the second step in the process: build your team. We will go into greater detail about who to select and how to structure the team in the next chapter as well as how to engage participants.

A traditional charter will include the following sections and may be modified to meet your specific project requirements:

Table 6.2

Project Charter – Key Components
1. Business problem statement:
2. Project focus:
3. Project vision and objectives:
4. Project guiding principles:
5. Risk of not implementing project:
6. Project sponsors, steering committee, key project team members:
7. Individual and team learning objectives:
8. High level scope:
9. High level deliverables:
10. Project assumptions and constraints:
11. High level schedule:
12. Interconnected projects:
13. Charter approval signatures:

Stories and Examples

In the next section we provide an example of how these tools have been used. Paul is a composite drawn from our experience with several clients and is the case study throughout the balance of the book to give you a realistic flavor of how each of these tools is used to support a transformation effort. Paul will complete each step in the process so you can see how tools and reflection questions are used to support transformation.

Sample Responses for Paul as a Strategist

In Section I, when we defined Developmental Perspective, we talked about the Strategist level and its ability to successfully lead complex change efforts. We believe it is helpful for you to read how someone with the Strategist perspective would look at this change effort, so Paul will be responding to reflection questions from the Strategist Developmental Perspective. Through our client work and teaching, we've found that giving examples of how each perspective uses these exercises to be especially insightful in the personal growth process. We have tried to capture Paul's internal thought process in these exercises in a way that is rare in a business context, but helpful for the purpose of professional development and leading organizational transformation.

Introduction to Paul

At age 42, Paul has recently has joined a global manufacturing firm as the CIO. On a daily basis he is involved in transforming the IT organization across multiple plants around the world. When he took the job, the organization had several computer systems and used Excel spreadsheets extensively. Through his analysis, he determined that implementing an enterprise resource planning (ERP) software system and upgrading servers would save the organization a large sum of money on the technology side. He partnered with his colleagues in the business units to determine that this transition would improve organizational efficiency (one of the company's strategic goals) and also improve the customer experience.

Paul is also actively involved in his own personal development journey. He has been working with a coach for a number of years while taking on large scale change efforts. He is now testing as a Strategist, so he is well qualified to lead the complicated change that he is proposing.

The first step in leading the transformation effort is to understand the foundation for the change effort (sample change foundation assessment). The following tool walks us through the analysis Paul uses to validate his initial hypothesis that implementing an ERP system and upgrading servers is in the best interest of the business and will significantly impact the strategic goal of improving operational efficiency.

If the project is approved based on the change foundation assessment, the organization will then complete the project charter. Since Paul was successful in advocating for his project, we included his completed Project Charter after the change foundation assessment.

Sample Change Foundation Assessment

Objective: The foundation assessment is designed to help you understand and clearly articulate why this project is being undertaken and serves as the basis for next steps in data collection. Another benefit this analysis provides is that it starts to build the foundation for the charter and the information that will be communicated in the awareness packages to new project team members and change network (people who support the project on a part-time or ad-hoc basis).

Data Source: Review of organizational documents such as vision and strategic plan and interviews with key stakeholders. After initial analysis, a business case was created to support the primary foundation for the transformation. (*These initial documents were refined during the data collection and analysis phase.*) A business case captures the business need for conducting the project. It generally explains the project objectives, project investment, expected outcomes, and business value at a minimum. For large, complex, and expensive projects, companies often invest in a thorough business case analysis before taking on the investment and risk of the project. For smaller projects, the business case can be accomplished through a more rudimentary analysis and simple documentation.

Organizational Vision: We are a thriving organization because our work creates thriving clients who build thriving communities

Strategic Goal: Improve organizational efficiency (strategic plan provides more specific details on how this is measured)

Project Objective:

- Implement new computer system – Enterprise resource planning (ERP)
- Centralize hardware and support services
- Adopt leading processes and/or best practices and standardize across multiple locations

Key Stakeholders:

- Executive leadership investing in the project
- Business units using the technology and changing work processes
- Corporate offices using the technology and changing work processes
- IT implementing and managing the new technology and changing their work processes
- Customers who will more often receive accurate and timely shipments
- Investor community who will receive higher financial returns after the business case is realized

Diagnostic activities have been used to confirm the situation:

- In-depth strategic planning and analysis project identified key opportunities
- Interviews with key stakeholders to validate the need
- Developed thorough business case (during the data collection and analysis phase)

Expected Changes:

- Computer systems
- Wide range of computer programs and manual processes
- Critical business processes
- Ability to adapt to change
- Where computers are located and how maintained
- Decision making processes and data available to make decisions
- Who makes decisions within organization and the level of decisions they make
- Move to disciplined process focus resulting in decreased level of autonomy and freedom in deciding how the job is done by individual locations

Consequences if changes are not implemented:

- Loss of market share as competitors make these changes and improve their performance
- Missed opportunity to improve competitive position within the industry
- Miss ROI targets
- Increased risk exposure
- Stock price impact
- Bonus/profit sharing impact
- Potential negative career impact for selected individuals

Approval - Who authorized the project?

- CEO
- CIO
- Business unit president

Project Motivation:

- Improve profitability
- Double the size of the business
- Reduce inventory costs
- Provide a platform to integrate new businesses
- Increase efficiency and effectiveness of the business
- Make company best place to work
- Improve customer experience (ease of business with us, improve order accuracy, and improve on-time delivery)

Implementation Activities:

- Educate leaders and change mindset about how to run the business
- Design processes that support overall business objectives
- Configure systems that support business objectives and streamline reporting
- Test system effectiveness
- Prepare people for change (communicate, create excitement and buy-in, train)
- Prepare human support infrastructure (job descriptions, appraisals, compensation and rewards, sourcing, training)
- Change long-term compensation systems to reinforce system, culture, and behavioral changes required for the system to succeed

Processes in scope:

- Order to Cash
- Procure to Pay (procurement and accounts payable)
- Marketing and Sales
- Plan to Produce (scheduling, i.e., planning and production

Resources:

- Staffing – project plan will be developed to specify number of internal staff members from each department
- Consulting support – proposals will be solicited for exact cost—ballpark estimate is a range from $x to $x to happen over the next 24-36 months to be clarified during detailed project planning phase
- Technology investment – to be clarified during proposal and detailed planning phase—range of investment is from $x to $x
- Leadership time to steer the project and serve as sponsors

Risk Management:

- System implementation will occur in phases
- Process improvement and standardization changes will occur in advance of system deployment to manage performance risk and accelerate the benefit of process standardization
- IT changes will happen quickly after proof of concept to address security/ disaster recovery related concerns (accelerate benefits of migrating off old systems that incur ongoing maintenance)

Sponsors:

- CIO
- Business Unit President
- VP Operations
- VP Purchasing
- Business Unit CFO

Outcomes upon project completion:

Using the business case, summarize the expected business outcomes and measures for the project

Table 6.3

State of the organization upon successful Implementation – populate using Strategic Plan		
Business Area	**Outcomes**	**Measures**
Business Operations	▪ Process changes to provide additional competitive advantage and more effective resource usage ▪ Business decisions based on accurate data	▪ ROI ▪ Profitability ▪ Customer satisfaction and retention ▪ Reduced inventory cost and investment
Technical	▪ Increased technical capabilities ▪ Centralized hardware ▪ Consolidation of many software tools into single end to end tool to run the business (one version of the truth) ▪ More accurate information in the desired format ▪ Increased focus on disaster recovery	▪ Number of manual vs. automated processes (inventory, etc.) ▪ Number of business opportunities with technical foundation
Human Aspects	▪ Increased ability to absorb change without losing focus ▪ Learn new business processes ▪ Learn new computer ▪ Develop additional business skills	▪ Speed of change acceptance ▪ Decreased productivity dip ▪ Accelerated learning curve ▪ Employee engagement results ▪ Retention
Leader	▪ Build skills necessary to successfully implement transformation ▪ Build innovative leadership capacity	▪ Feedback from others ▪ Change successful ▪ Positioned for future change success
Culture	▪ Identify culture changes needed to successfully implement and sustain the organizational benefits associated with change	▪ Culture survey results ▪ New culture supportive of this and successive changes

Project Charter

We, as a leadership team, reviewed the change foundation assessment against the other projects presented during the planning session and approved this as one of the efforts we will work on this year. Based on that foundation, we created the following charter to specify what would be expected from this project. Our goal was to present a high-level description and success measures giving enough information for the team to know what to do, while at the same time providing enough latitude for them to make appropriate decisions about how to accomplish the goals. The charter below reflects the second phase of a large enterprise transformation project. As mentioned above, we decided to break the implementation into multiple projects to minimize risk and impact to the organization. As you are creating the charter, it will be important to consider how the project will be structured and fit within or operate outside of the traditional hierarchy.

According to Kotter in a November 2012, *Harvard Business Review* article:

> *"Although traditional hierarchies and processes—which together form a company's "operating system"—are optimized for day-to-day business, they can't handle the challenges of mounting complexity and rapid change. The solution is a second operating system, devoted to the design and implementation of strategy that uses an agile, network-like structure and a very different set of processes. The new operating system continually assesses the business, the industry, and the organization, and reacts with greater agility, speed, and creativity than the existing one. It complements rather than overburdens the hierarchy, thus freeing the latter to do what it's optimized to do. It actually makes enterprises easier to run and accelerates strategic change."*

We agree with this premise for many projects—especially those that are addressing adaptive challenges. In these cases, the hierarchy may preclude the team from developing solutions that are sufficiently comprehensive. If your project will operate outside of the traditional hierarchy, it will be important to spell that out in the charter and also select people who have the capacity to work in an agile environment that in some cases functions more like a network than a hierarchy. This is where we build on the innovative leadership framework. Leaders with the Individualist

Developmental Perspective will be more effective in this alternate operating system than those who have a center of gravity at Achiever or earlier. We will continue to explore team selection in the next chapter.

If you are implementing a series of interconnected projects like that referenced in this example, you may want to create a network structure where multiple projects are managed collectively. In traditional project management terms there are multiple projects that combine to form a program. This may still be the case but the management structure may be less traditionally hierarchical and more fluid, using more agile governing approaches. One of these approaches is called Holacracy. Holacracy is a comprehensive practice for structuring, governing, and running an organization. It replaces today's top-down predict-and-control paradigm with a new way of distributing power and achieving control. It is a new "operating system" which instills rapid evolution in the core processes of an organization. While it is beyond the scope of this book, we mention it here to let you know there are well-tested approaches to governance that are designed for agile, networked environments and structures. More information can be found at www.holacracy.org

Sample Charter

1. Business Problem Statement

The organization is not meeting its overall efficiency goals. To protect privacy of the organizations who contributed to this charter, we are not revealing details of the problem. At a high level the problems included:

- High price of maintaining decentralized hardware
- Multiple software systems that required extensive labor to reconcile data
- High inventory cost including spoilage and carrying costs
- High inventory investment
- High inventory storage costs
- Inefficient processes
- Customer dissatisfaction caused by missed deliveries
- Stock price flat for three years—market sending signals that our competitors are becoming more efficient than we are; losing industry leader positioning

2. Project Focus

Ensure that key organizational changes occur in coordination with the second phase of Enterprise Resource Planning (ERP) System implementation. Many of these changes will need to occur prior to the deployment of the ERP, necessitating a separate project to ensure appropriate focus and control.

There are five initial areas of focus for the project. They are listed below along with a brief description of how each area supports the overall objective of the organizational change project.

Enterprise Resource Planning Education and Training – This activity will help prepare the management team, project team, and key individuals within the organization to make "key decisions" regarding business processes, organizational structures, job design, and software configuration. This training will teach them a new way of thinking about, and running, key elements of their operation.

Purchase Order Due Date Adherence – A major component of the ERP has already been implemented. Business process changes are necessary to ensure there are no past due dates on purchase orders in order to ensure future functionality of the ERP. This activity will create the processes and structure necessary to support and reinforce the behavioral changes required to increase the reliability of purchase order dates.

Inventory Analysis – An understanding of leading practices to segment inventory items into classifications will be provided to project team members and the initial segmentation will be conducted. This activity will create the processes and structure necessary to support and reinforce the behavioral changes required to complete this type of analysis on a periodic basis following the deployment of the ERP System.

Forecasting – More robust forecasting is necessary to move the organization from a "reactive" organization to a "planning" organization. The high-level business process for forecasting will be developed and validated to help move the company toward the goal of running the business based on one forecast. All required planning models will also be identified and representative models will be developed. Future projects will involve developing all planning models.

Change Management – This activity will focus on identifying and tracking key changes to the organization required to support the deployment of the ERP.

This includes developing an impact analysis, creating a high level approach, creating deliverables to help execute the change management process, facilitating behavioral changes, coordinating activities with stakeholders, and tracking actions and metrics to ensure that the desired results will be achieved. Support to improve organizational effectiveness will be provided as needed to the Enterprise Systems Project Team.

3. Project Vision and Objectives

The following are the objectives of the Organizational Transformation project:

- Deliver executive-level ERP education and training and change executive-level approach to thinking about and running the business
- Assign ABC inventory segmentation class codes and develop recommendations for applying planning parameters based on ABC values
- Define new business processes, including tracking metrics, to improve due date accuracy by eliminating past-due purchase orders
- Define forecasting processes and planning models
- Identify key changes related to the organizational transformation project, along with supporting action plans to address the change requirements
- Create deliverables from the project plan to facilitate behavioral changes within the broad organization
- Develop a project plan
- Increase change readiness within the organization
- Support the Enterprise Systems Project Team to increase team effectiveness
- Make recommendations for interim process changes. Determine which changes can be made early to provide early wins and which changes <u>must</u> be made early to reduce implementation risk

4. Guiding Principles

- Human change management is not a separate component of Enterprise Change—it is the heart of the effort. The Enterprise Project, itself, is change. As a result of this project, the organization will fundamentally change the way it does business. Therefore, every component of the project must include change management and coaching

- The change must be **led and owned** by employees
- Capacity for change must be enhanced (volume of change should be managed, feedback and performance support should be provided; training, coaching, and capacity building should be provided)
- Involvement in the change effort must be increased to develop and maintain commitment (a critical mass of people from multiple geographies, companies, and product lines must be involved to provide substantive input to the design and redesign of processes)
- Given that deployment of new processes, roles and technology often result in short-term productivity loss, our goal is to minimize this loss and accelerate the achievement of a long-term gain in productivity. Clarifying this as an expectation upfront makes it a "safer" environment in which to institute the change without folks getting unduly concerned about short-term losses

5. **Risk Associated with the Project**

- Leadership unprepared to lead transformation project causing costly project delays, increased labor and consulting costs, and loss of employee confidence and engagement
- Focus on getting the job done rather than following the processes will create downstream problems with every element of the business
- People resist change because they are not sufficiently informed and trained—another factor that reduces a sense of security; hence, willingness to try new behaviors and activities. This resistance could adversely impact every element of the business and its ability to achieve the business case
- Unable to place orders and ship products on Day 1 of implementation
- Inventory not available to support production on Day 1 of implementation
- Organization employees undertrained and overwhelmed by the changes, not performing their jobs properly, adversely impacting customers, inventory, and safety stock
- Risk mitigation strategies

6. **Project Sponsors, Steering Committee, and Project Team Members**

- Business Sponsor:
- Steering Committee Members:
- Business Team Lead:
- Project Manager:
- IT Lead:
- Change Network Lead:
- Change Management Lead:
- Coaching Lead:

7. **Individual and Team Learning Objectives**

- Build individual and organizational expertise in supply chain management and materials management
  - Sales & Operations Planning
  - Inventory Management
  - Forecasting
  - Master Scheduling
  - Customer Planning and Satisfaction
- Build expertise in leveraging ERP system to promote organizational efficiency
- Build ERP expertise in IT

8. **High Level Scope**

The Organizational Change project focuses on providing the necessary processes and structure to begin making required organizational changes. It will also provide the structure and support for realizing the completion of the following business process changes: (1) Purchase Order Due Dates, (2) Inventory Management, and (3) Forecasting.

The structure and support will be provided by enabling and facilitating ERP education and training and mentoring sessions for individuals who will be most impacted within the company as well as in the identification of key organizational changes, job design changes, and long-lead time change impact items. The identified items will be closely linked to the Enterprise Systems project to ensure that required organizational changes are supported by configuration decisions. Barriers and enablers to change will be identified and the process of increasing change readiness will be launched. In many cases, behavioral changes associated with business process changes will be facilitated.

Project team members will work with executives and managers, as well as with the Enterprise Systems project team as needed to ensure that: (1) identified changes will be supported by the business leaders; (2) process and job design changes will be integrated into the business flows; (3) the design of processes and jobs is supported by the ERP configuration; and (4) the timing of deploying changes will support the development and deployment schedule. The Organizational Transformation project will not be involved with the configuration of the ERP.

Organizational change management activities for future initiatives will be budgeted and scheduled as part of those projects.

9. High Level Project Deliverables

- Delivered executive level ERP education and training sessions. These sessions will occur on a bi-weekly schedule. Session topics and planned dates are listed in this Charter

- Documented business processes and the training necessary to eliminate past-due purchase orders including processes and metrics to evaluate compliance

- Agreed-upon and documented guidelines for segmenting all items (raw materials, intermediate products, and finished goods) using the ABC value class analysis approach

- Recommendations for which order policies should be applied to different inventory classes of items

- High-level business process for how forecasting will be performed and reliability measured in the future

- Initial inventory of organizational changes related to the Organizational Change initiatives as well as changes required by long-lead time items within the Enterprise Systems Project

- Change Management approach

- Coaching approach/plan

- Change Readiness Assessments of key stakeholders

- Detailed change management plans for the ERP Solution

- Documented recommendations on a long-term organizational structure that supports Enterprise Resource Planning leading practices

- Initial Change Item Detail forms completed for each identified change, listing impact, stakeholders, and action plans

- Change related deliverables as identified in the change management plan

- Coaching deliverables as identified in the coaching approach/plan

- Support the Enterprise Project Team as appropriate in addressing team effectiveness issues

- Organizational change and process improvement recommendations

10. Project Assumptions & Constraints

Assumptions

- The project has Executive Management support including participation in ERP education and training sessions and a commitment to seeing the implementation through to completion

- Business managers will be available in a timely manner to validate the key organizational change decisions required by this project

- Personnel will be available to support this project as defined by the detailed project plan

- ERP leading practices will be evaluated when determining future organizational processes and structure

- Any change to the agreed-upon scope, schedule and/or budget will be managed by the Change Control process

- The project team will have the ability to extract required data from the mainframe and the ERP system to support the Purchases Order Due Date Adherence, Inventory Analysis, and Forecasting activities
- Multiple project and business team members will enroll in APICS classes and achieve a mastery of the APICS Body of Knowledge
- Project team members will complete extensive training in ERP configuration in time to support the objectives of this Project
- Project team members and executive managers will accept the ABCD Checklist as a framework for improving business performance
- Members of the project team will work with members of the project team to ensure coordination and alignment of effort

Constraints

- This project will be governed by the agreed-upon project and resource plans
- The project cost and schedule may be impacted if business and organizational change decisions are not made in a timely manner and/or do not support the project plan

11. Interconnected Projects

- Phase II is a project designed to support Phase I of the ERP implementation
- Phase II will serve as the foundation for Phase III the implementation of the planning and scheduling modules

12. Key Deliverable Schedule (focused on training deliverables)

The following schedule is subject to change. Please contact the project manager for any updates.

Table 6.4

Topic	Training Date
Inventory Analysis	
Supply Orders	
Demand Orders	
Forecasting	
Master Scheduling	
Material Planning	
Order Entry and Processing	
Sales & Operations Planning	

13. Charter Approval Signature

By signing, sponsors acknowledge that they understand and support the content of this document as it existed when they signed.

Table 6.5

Name	Project Role	Signature	Date
	Executive Program Director		
	Project Sponsor		
	Steering Committee Member		
	Steering Committee Member		
	Steering Committee Member		
	Steering Committee Member		

Innovative Leadership Reflection Questions

To help you create a compelling vision and sense of urgency, it is timve to further clarify your own beliefs using reflection questions. As a reminder, this is an opportunity to practice innovative leadership by considering how your change plan will affect your intentions, actions, culture, and systems. The questions for "What do I think/believe?" reflect your intentions. The questions "What do I do?" reflect your actions. The questions "What do we believe?" reflect culture. The questions "How do we do this?" reflect systems. Thus, we designed this exercise to help you start practicing innovative leadership as you create your vision and define your direction.

The table contains several questions for each domain to be applicable to a broad range of projects. We recommend you **choose two to four questions** from each domain that best apply to your specific situation.

Table 6.6

QUESTIONS TO GUIDE THE LEADER AND ORGANIZATION

What do I think / believe?
- How do I see myself in the future?
- How does my view of myself impact my ability to participate in this change?
- How do I see our organization within the larger environment (ranging from the company to the global environment)?
- What are the connections between possible business futures and my personal mission, passion, and economic goals (Hedgehog Principle in *Good to Great*)?
- Why do I believe this change is urgent and necessary?
- What do I need to change about myself to lead the change successfully?
- What will I need to change about my leadership style to lead an adaptive change and corresponding business transformation?
- What is motivating me to make this change?

What do I do?

- How do I gather input from key stakeholders to incorporate into the "vision" and "sense of urgency" statements?
- How do I consider best practices when setting the vision and communicating a sense of urgency?
- How do I synthesize competing goals and commitments to create a vision that works for the organization and is supported by multiple stakeholders?
- How do I translate the vision into long- and short-term timelines?
- How do I incorporate specific tangible goals into the timelines?
- Do I allocate the funds required to meet the project requirements and timelines?
- How will I model an appropriate response to the sense of urgency by my actions?
- What actions do I take to respond to the urgent concerns of my stakeholders?
- How will I encourage the segment(s) most likely to change without ignoring others?
- How will I explain the impact of change in a manner consistent with our culture and values?
- What stories can I use from our corporate folklore to illustrate prior examples of urgency and positive outcome?
- How can I convey messages that use emotion (personal stories) and external sources to demonstrate urgency?
- What systems must change immediately to develop a high impact organization?
- How do I set the tone that it is safe to try new things and make reasonable mistakes as we transform?

What do we believe?

- What are the organizational guiding principles?
- How does the organization see itself in the context of the larger community?
- What do we believe we stand for? What do we believe about how we should behave to accomplish what we stand for?
- How does our organizational vision fit within the larger context, i.e. community, industry?
- If you are making a change in a department of a large organization, how does the vision support the overall organization's vision?
- How do we create a belief that the vision will help the organization succeed within the larger community and also help the community succeed?
- What do my stakeholders see as urgent? Important? How does this perception vary across stakeholder groups?
- Do the employees see the need to change the culture to be more successful?
- What about the culture must change to support more effective business operations?

How do we do this?

- What is our process for determining the shared vision and values for the organization?
- What is the process for clarifying and documenting our guiding principles?
- How does the organization develop its vision taking the greater economic conditions into account (by combining an analysis of trends, our strengths, and market demand)?
- How do we understand and incorporate stakeholder priorities into the vision?
- How do we cascade the shared vision of possible futures (realistic and wild card options) to all levels of the organization?
- How do we translate the vision into a measurable work plan with goals? Who owns the specific goals?
- What measures help the organization determine progress toward goals? How do we track and report progress to these goals?
- What types of assessments are or can be performed to quantitatively determine the urgency and options? Are the assessments comprehensive in nature? Do they include input from stakeholders inside and outside of the business?
- What are the barriers and enablers that will impact success (legal, financial, building, staffing mix)?
- What systems need to be changed immediately to remove short-term barriers?
- What resources are required to succeed and how will we secure them?
- What measures should we track to understand the employees' sense of urgency so we can manage their level of distress (creating an environment that promotes change without overwhelming people)?
- How do I measure and report to stakeholders on the items they said were important?

Next, Paul will answer two to four reflection questions from each of the four dimensions above.

What do I think / believe?

- ***What do I need to change about myself to lead the change successfully?***

While I believe I am an effective leader, I test as a Strategist on the Developmental Perspective Assessment (MAP). I have gotten feedback that people do not always understand what I am doing and why. Because I see the bigger picture where others do not, communicating with me frustrates them. I need to make sure I am talking to people at their level because we will be asking them to make changes that seem like nothing to me, but to them may be a very big deal. I guess you could say I need to get better at understanding how the change impacts them—because if it were me, I would think it is not so tough.

■ *What will I need to change about my leadership style to lead an adaptive change and corresponding business transformation?*

By adaptive change I think you mean a change that requires me to change who I am as a leader, as well as the tasks I do on a daily basis. Well, an integrated system that can be seen across the enterprise means how I run the IT department will need to change. At this point I am not really sure how this will impact my daily tasks. I hear from others who have implemented a similar system that the process is terribly disruptive and we will have some turnover as people who do not "get it" will leave. What I think I need to change most is my ability (as I referenced above) to be more patient with people going through, what are for them, very large changes. I tend to treat people with a high level of autonomy, expecting them to figure things out. It sounds like I will need to be more directly involved at a granular level for a while until people are able to settle into new ways of doing things. Because I tend to see the bigger picture more than most, I will need to communicate what I see in ways that are helpful to others rather than expecting them to just figure it out. This may be a significant adjustment for me. I also need to remember that creating a safe environment for people to change is critical. If they are worried at the onset about failure, they will be far less willing to engage in difficult new behaviors and activities.

What do I do?

■ *How do I synthesize competing goals and commitments to create a vision that works for the organization and is supported by multiple stakeholders?*

I know that our people are really busy. Because I was the one who had to create the Change Foundation Assessment, I already talked to our key stakeholders and had to explain to the corporate leadership team why this vision is right and why it is *right now* (sense of urgency). What I learned through this process is that our competitors are already ahead of us and seeing strong results. If we want to maintain our competitive advantage, we need to get on this as aggressively as possible without taking on unnecessary risk. I have the support of the senior leadership team, now I need to get the IT department on board—the president of the business unit will work with his organization to ensure they are onboard. I will play a supporting role to him—part of this will be explaining some of the technical details they do not understand, but that present a high risk if not resolved quickly.

I also need to remember that we report to a board of directors. We need to keep them informed and involved when appropriate. This project can only succeed if our Board buys in and provides continual support.

■ *How will I model an appropriate response to the sense of urgency by my actions?*

I realize people look to me to set the tone for the change. I will need to make sure that I am not only dedicating time to the project but also being visible in what I do. This is not my style—having to make sure people know that I am being a role model. I kind of want them to just believe in me. So, my plan is to talk about what we are doing and what I am doing in all of my staff meetings. I will also integrate talking points about project activities and how it will impact us in my weekly e-mail to staff. I know we will be taking on lots of additional workload and we will have consultants sharing our already packed space.

The other thing I probably need to think about is deciding which of my tasks I can delegate to the directors working for me since this project will take a significant chunk of my time at the beginning as we select a vendor and create the plan.

What do we believe?

■ *How does the organization see itself in the context of the larger community?*

We have always seen ourselves as an industry leader and, also, as a big supporter of the community. We are highly respected by our Board, business owners, and community leaders alike. This respect is based on our highly ethical business practices. We treat people fairly and have not had a lay-off in the company's history. We are seen by many as best in class but I personally think that if we are not careful, we will quickly fall behind. The broadly shared belief that we are better than others can be dangerous if it allows us to sit back while our competitors become more successful in the market we pioneered.

■ *Do employees see the need to change the culture to be more successful?*

Our employees love the current culture. We hire good people and they work hard. With the new system, we are moving much closer to an automated, scheduled, and managed-by-the-numbers culture. There are lots of people who will not like this as they will think they are being monitored by "big brother." Managers will not want to move to a more structured approach and many employees really like the pitch in and get it done culture that seems, unfortunately, to also have limited accountability. So, I anticipate many people thinking that they will lose the family feel and become just another corporate entity. I understand the feeling, so my challenge is to help people see the benefit of this way of operating and also to find ways to maintain the sense of family and care that keeps people engaged and committed to the company.

How do we do this?

■ *What is our process for determining the shared vision and values for the organization?*

Our vision and values were set by our founder. We are a company that is very proud of its heritage and its values have served us well. We have not changed them since our inception. The question of values will be a tough one. I do not yet know the answer, but will our original values need to be changed to support the changes? We were founded 75 years ago and the values during that era were much different than they are now. We want to honor our legacy yet position ourselves to thrive for generations to come. I trust our management team and know we will have some serious discussions about questions this system change will cause us to address that we have not had to face in the past.

■ *What measures should we track to understand the employees' sense of urgency so we can manage their level of distress—creating an environment that promotes change without overwhelming people?*

Since the IT organization will be taking on a large part of the project implementation role, I know I need to manage the employee concerns with bandwidth. I have a few ideas about this. I want to do a simple quarterly climate survey—it could even be a simple Resilience assessment to see how people are taking care of themselves. We could then aggregate the individual results to see what we look like as a group and at the same time give people individual feedback about their own progress. We can pace the project a bit to adjust to employee needs, but the other side of the equation is what can we put in place now that helps employees build their personal capacity. We are a health-oriented company so most people have access to a gym and those at headquarters have healthy food available. There are other things we can do to make the environment more effective. We will conduct team building sessions when we kick off new teams to help people understand the requirements and also build supportive connections with one another. I believe having a best friend at work really helps Resilience and employee engagement. I will need to look at other opportunities as we go along to help individuals build their personal Resilience and capacity to navigate and absorb change.

Finally, as leaders, we need to make every effort to help people feel safe to try new behaviors and make mistakes at every step in the process. This security will allow them to engage and will significantly reduce resistance.

Now that you have seen Paul's reflection questions and his use of some foundation tools, if you are working on a change, this is the time for you to consider how you might put these or similar tools to work. *If you are like most leaders you will be tempted to complete the templates and skip the reflection questions—we strongly suggest you resist that urge.* Part of the process of becoming a leader with the Developmental Perspective of Individualist or Strategist is cultivating the ability to reflect on a regular basis. We regularly hear from leaders who say they do not have any time in their day to stop and consider the broader picture. These reflection questions give you that opportunity.

Throughout this chapter we have provided templates, processes, and examples for you to use to create a compelling vision and sense of urgency. You will use the foundation assessment to clarify the high level details of your project and as the foundation for your charter. From there you will proceed to create a high-level project charter. We also introduced the concept that the project team may work outside of the traditional hierarchical structure using a network-based structure that connects multiple change projects. The remainder of Section II focuses on the actual process involved to bring your compelling vision into existence.

CHAPTER 7

Build Team

Fig. 7.1 Innovative Leadership Development Process

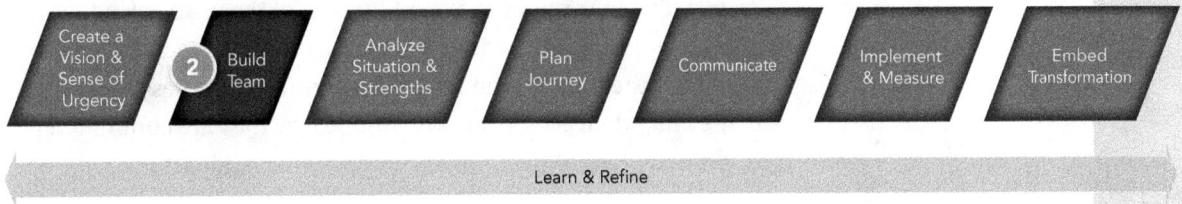

Create a Vision & Sense of Urgency | 2 Build Team | Analyze Situation & Strengths | Plan Journey | Communicate | Implement & Measure | Embed Transformation

Learn & Refine

Build Team

Step two in the process involves determining the best people for the team, then focusing on building the team.

The first part is identifying who will be involved in the transition and in which roles. ***This is both a vote for who is, as well as who is not, part of the transformation or on the leadership team***. So, if you are selecting a team, it will be important to understand the selection criteria. Some criteria to consider are: subject matter experience and skills, ability to create buy-in, perceived leadership and influence in the organization, Developmental Perspective (introduced in Chapter 2), and behavioral qualities that will allow participants to function well as part of a team. If you have leadership issues, it is important to address them early. If there are people on the leadership team who will undermine the project success, you want to make the difficult decisions early. Often these people are asked to join the team because they have critical knowledge and relationships, or they are retained in roles that will not impact overall success. These are never easy actions to take but do become an issue of managing risk as well as engagement for high-cost/high-impact projects.

The second part is building the team. By building the team, we do not mean sending an e-mail informing leaders that they now have an "extra duty;" it means dedicating time to helping team members truly understand the urgency and vision of the project and getting them excited about the impact they can make on the organization through their participation. They need to understand what is involved. After team members are selected, they will engage in team building activities to learn how to work with one another effectively on a high-demand, high-stress project.

Depending on the project size and complexity, you will likely have multiple teams. They could include:

- Steering committee - responsible for overall project oversight and success. It champions the effort, shows visible support, monitors project success, evaluates risk, and participates in major decisions

- Sponsors - responsible for providing overall support of the change (in the organization as a whole and in distributed locations at their site or location). Their actions will set the tone for the site's implementation success. If Sponsors do not "walk the talk," their employees will not believe they are committed to the project and the success of the implementation will be impacted

- Project Team - the team of people directly involved in the daily activities of accomplishing the project. For large scale projects, key members of the project team are reassigned to the project in full time roles

- Extended Team (also known as the change agent network) - people supportive of the change and credible within the organization; enlisted to help people impacted by the project understand and accept the changes they will experience

- Subject Matter Experts – ad hoc participants involved on an as needed basis because of their expertise

Selection Criteria

Team members are selected across a range of criteria. When change is enterprise-wide, the steering committee and the project team should be selected to represent every location and line of business impacted by the change. Managing change is a challenging task. It requires highly-skilled and motivated individuals working together to achieve the business objective. Key members across all teams should be chosen with the following competencies:

- **Performance:** Is seen as an expert in their current position. Can set aside personal agendas, desires, and biases that might hinder the success of the project

- **Communication:** Has excellent communication skills and is comfortable speaking with all levels and functions across the organization

- **Teamwork:** Can develop a high level of teamwork with key players in this implementation. Is a team player and is comfortable leading or following as necessary

- ■ **Credibility:** Must have a successful history in the organization with no political liabilities
- ■ **Trust:** Must act and speak in ways to facilitate trusting relationship with sponsors and targets
- ■ **Culture:** Has knowledge of multiple cultures within business units and locations
- ■ **Commitment:** Will demonstrate understanding and commitment to the overall enterprise changes. Must understand how project supports overall changes and acts as a champion within the organization at all levels to communicate and support project success and realization of business benefits
- ■ **Innovative Leadership:** There are several elements of innovative leadership that are critical to lead a large complex project. The leader's Developmental Perspective (introduced in Chapter 2 of this book) must be aligned with the task. Additionally, the leadership behaviors must be aligned with the project expectations. For complex adaptive change, most steering committee members and project team leads should have a center of gravity of Individualist or higher on the Developmental Perspective scale. This will allow them to manage complex adaptive change using a structure outside of the hierarchy
- ■ **Commitment to personal development:** As a leader, you will need to innovate how you lead in conjunction with the transformation within the organization. Must be willing to engage in coaching and development activities

After you select your team members, it will be important to communicate expectations and build the group into a team with a clear plan with specific expectations. Following is an example of a high-level sponsor plan. These plans will summarize individual expectations of each role. You will want a similar plan for each of the teams (using the previous list or other variations of teams).

In addition to creating a charter, it is important to get everyone together to kick-off or launch the team. We realize that in a global organization this may not be possible and may need to be handled by teleconference. At minimum, this session should include the following:

- ■ **On the task side:**
  - ■ Clear performance expectations
  - ■ Clear understanding of measures

- Understanding participant benefits for taking on this role (this could be company benefit in the case of senior leaders who are often compensated by bonus and is often different than the project team member who may be building skills toward promotion)
- Understanding sense of urgency—what is in it for them

■ **On the relationship side it will be important to:**

- Understand personality type and/or leadership competency of individuals and how they best contribute
- Understand the "personality type" or leadership competency of the group so you understand how you fit with the group—your strengths, as well as how to handle potential challenges
- Establish how you want to work together
- Understand individual strengths
- Begin to develop supportive alliances and friendships based on mutual interest, strengths, and trust

Tools

One of the first steps in this phase is having each person identify their "draft picks" using this worksheet or other format. The purpose of this process is to identify who would be a best fit against the selection criteria for those you select.

Table 7.1

Selection Matrix									
Criteria	Functional Expertise	Communication	Teamwork	Credibility	Trust	Culture	Commitment	Developmental Perspective	Commitment to Develop
	Y/N	Y/N	Y/N	Y/N	Y/N	Y/N	Y/N	(Level)	Y/N
Steering Committee									
Chair									
Member									
Member									

Sponsors									
Project Team Members									
Project Manager									
Team Leads									

Team Charter

After you identify who is on the teams, you will want to create plans for each of the teams explaining their responsibilities and measures and how you will work to engage them in the project. Following is a table showing a sample of items that may be included. Different organizations will include different components, but this list serves as a solid starting point. According to the McKinsey research about the top six tactics for change success referenced at the beginning of the book, one is establishing well-defined stretch targets. By creating individual and team objectives, learning objectives and responsibilities, participants understand what is expected and how they will meet their goals.

Table 7.2

Team objectives:
Team learning objectives:
Major deliverables:
Responsibilities:
Engagement:
Timing:
Measure of success:
Resource requirements:

After the charters are created, it will be important to have a team building or launch. Among tools that will support this process will be a team assessment. Most teams find that they benefit greatly by using a skilled facilitator—who is not part of the team—to plan and facilitate the session. This person should have a strong ability to understand and navigate complex team dynamics. Tools for the session will include:

- Discussion of objectives and roles and responsibilities to clarify the work of the team
- Team dynamics are also an important component of the kick-off
  - Enneagram individual and composite team assessment
  - LCP or other 360 individual and team composite assessment

Stories and examples

When organizations are too large to have all locations actively involved, you will want to consider how you group locations such as regions or countries. When you cannot include everyone, include those who are most impacted.

In selecting your team, you will want to leverage the assessment results—this is one of the areas in which the transformation steps will be happening concurrently. You may want to begin assessing your leaders using key assessment tools prior to finalizing team selection if you have questions, for example, about Developmental Perspective.

If you do not have leaders who are at the Individualist or Strategist Developmental Perspective (which is unlikely in large complex organizations) you can leverage consultants and/or you may have people at these later Developmental Perspectives who are not on the leadership team. If this is the case, you will want to position these people as trusted advisors to the sponsor team rather than voting members of the team.

Let's return to Paul as he selects his sponsor team. Paul has evaluated the range of leaders within his organization and has made sure he has people from most functional units and locations and has at least one person at the Strategist Developmental Perspective (which is him). This team selection process is a tough one because he needs to attend to skills, behavioral characteristics, region, Developmental Perspective, and team size. He wanted a team of twelve or fewer. He ended up with ten people he thought would be very effective as the steering committee.

He then worked with that steering committee to select the project team and the sponsor team. He will look to the sponsors to select the extended team as the project progresses and to determine how to best leverage the extended team's involvement.

Following is a subset of the sponsor plan Paul worked with the steering committee to create.

Sponsor Plan

Objective: The Sponsorship plan addresses the need to have executives throughout the organization leading the change. It will serve as the activity road map. Sponsors will help each group of users understand and embrace the change program and the business goals driving the program. Sponsors will ensure that the planned changes deliver the intended benefits for the organization.

Sponsors are responsible for providing overall support of the change at their site and their actions will set the tone for the site's implementation success.

Major Deliverables:
- Create site-specific sponsorship plans
- Facilitate sponsor education material and action plans
- Conduct ongoing follow-up with sponsors
- Create metrics to gauge change readiness
- Resource requirements

Table 7.3

Activity	When	Message	Primary Objective
Steering Committee Action			

Steering Committee Meets with Site Sponsor		■ Explain expectations for:
		  ▪ Participation (specific behaviors)
		  ▪ Results
		  ▪ Level of authority, accountability, and control
		  ▪ Project Involvement
		  ▪ Rewards/consequences
			■ Create a mutual understanding of responsibility, commitment, and authority for implementing the project
			■ Define consequences of success and failure

Create Steering Committee Video		■ Explain benefits of the project ■ Explain how project links to other organizational objectives	■ Create a consistent message of executive support and explain why this is important to overall organizational performance
Site / Location Sponsor (for projects that have multiple locations)			
Sponsor Initial Meeting	Jan.	■ Interview to determine implementation history and what should be done differently on this project ■ Determine what the site manager wants to get from this implementation (business benefits and what keeps him up at night) ■ Discuss specific action steps and determine type of support we can provide ■ Discuss best practices and/or lessons learned to shape their thinking (based on data)	■ Understand site-specific barriers and create a plan to manage these ■ Understand motivators to craft messages and solutions that address specific concerns ■ Begin to create sponsor action plan ■ Build understanding of actions necessary to create success
Site Sponsor Meeting with Direct Reports	Feb.	■ Administer Change Foundation Scorecard and score in the group ■ Discuss specific action steps for change success ■ Create an action plan	■ Create an understanding of infrastructure necessary for change success ■ Develop action plan to address open issues
Site Sponsor Kick-off Site Steering Committee	Feb.	■ Conduct site steering committee meeting and discuss expectations of project, reporting, expectations for level of authority and desired involvement	■ Set the expectation that this project is critical to company success, clarify expectations, measures, and involvement

Site Sponsor Kick-off Implementation Team	May	■ Attend and present at the implementation team kick-off meeting
		  • Discuss importance of the project, what he expects of them and what they can expect of him
		  • Motivational
			■ Set the expectation that this project is critical to company success, clarify expectations, measures, and involvement
			■ Build momentum and commitment

Site Sponsor Meet with Teams Monthly for Status and Support	Monthly/ bi-weekly	■ Track progress, make decisions, approve high level direction	■ Show support ■ Validate progress ■ Take corrective action
Site Sponsor Kick-off General Roll-out Session(s)	June – Oct.	■ Attend and present at the Overall Site Kick-Off meeting(s) • Discuss importance of the project, what he expects of them and what they can expect of him ■ Motivational	■ Set the expectation that this project is critical to their success, clarify expectations, measures, and involvement ■ Build momentum and commitment
Site Sponsor Discusses Project in Ongoing Company Meetings	Ongoing	■ Present project status and what to expect	■ Move entire organization from aware that this is happening to an understanding and clarity about how they will contribute
Site Sponsor Publicly Acknowledges Wins	TBD	■ Acknowledge contribution and accomplishments of the project team	■ Build momentum and commitment ■ Give people an incentive to participate ■ Create understanding of benefits of the project
Monthly Status Call with Project PMO	Monthly	■ Status update two-way ■ People management: how are they doing and how are we managing their careers	■ Build understanding and commitment ■ Identify barriers and address issues ■ Provide career opportunities to project team members to build commitment
Measure Change Readiness	Monthly July – Oct.	■ Use Change Foundation Scorecard and Change Readiness Scorecard ■ Refine action plan ■ Measure progress on plan	■ Establish baseline ■ Determine corrective action ■ Track action items

Innovative Leadership Reflection Questions

To help you define who should be involved in the project, it is time to further clarify your direction using reflection questions. These questions are organized to reflect the four domains introduced in Section I. As a reminder, this is an opportunity to practice innovative leadership by considering how your change plan will affect changes in your intentions, actions, culture, and systems. These questions are arranged to help you explore each of these domains. The questions for "What do I think/believe?" reflect your intentions. The questions "What do I do?" reflect your actions. The questions "What do we believe?" reflect culture. The questions "How do we do this?" reflect systems. Thus, we designed this exercise to help you start practicing innovative leadership as you create your vision and define your direction.

The table contains several questions for each domain to be applicable to a broad range of projects. We recommend you **choose two to four questions** from each domain that best apply to your specific situation.

Table 7.4

QUESTIONS TO GUIDE THE LEADER AND ORGANIZATION

What do I think / believe?
- Do I believe the change is good for those I am inviting to participate?
- How will my behaviors and beliefs impact others' success?
- Do I believe the people on the teams are being positioned for success?
- Do I believe participating in this project will be helpful for the careers of the people involved?
- Do I believe we have key leaders involved who will interfere with project success including demotivating employees on the project team?

What do I do?
- How do I determine and communicate the criteria for "right" people on the team? ("Right" includes character traits, innate capabilities, skills, and knowledge.)
- How do I place the "right" people in charge of the biggest opportunity (not the biggest problem)? How do I recruit them for this personal and business transformation?
- What comments and actions will demonstrate my belief that change is possible?
- Am I looking for opportunities to visibly support the project as events unfold?
- What am I doing to retain the participants in the company and on the project?
- How do I lead a team based on the task at hand? Am I focused sufficiently on running the business while still attending to the change (personal and organizational)?
- Do I need to make difficult staffing decisions that would involve removing (not selecting) key leaders for roles?

What do we believe?

- What are the social and cultural norms that dictate who should be leading the project?
- How do we use the project as an opportunity to test new behaviors and demonstrate their positive impact on the organization?
- Do current social and cultural norms still fit for where we are going?
- Do people leading the change have the right support to change the culture as appropriate?
- How do we engage people in our organization to promote involvement and adoption?

How do we do this?

- What are the key skills and behaviors necessary for the organization to transform?
- What are the gaps between our current staff and the staff needed to support transformation? Does the organization have people available with the right skills and behaviors?
- What is the best combination of approaches to allow us to meet staffing needs, including hiring, reassignments, temps, and consultants?
- Does our hiring strategy support attracting the type of people we are trying to find? Are we asking the right questions in the interview process to select people who can successfully implement change?
- What trust building activities can we conduct to improve team dynamics?
- What measures should we track to reinforce desired team behaviors? Personal and professional changes?
- If the transformation is a long one, how are team members rewarded for their effort and risk? What happens if a team member does not thrive in the project environment?
- Am I communicating what stakeholders believe is important to the team?
- What are the processes that support selection of team members? Are they formalized? What are the criteria that will support team success?

In preparation for selecting team members, Paul answered the reflection questions. He anticipated that he would need to make some tough decisions and knew that this reflection process would help him think through some of those issues in advance of the meeting at which team members would be "drafted."

What do I think / believe?

- *Do I believe participating in this project will be helpful for the careers of the people involved? Do I believe the change is good for those I am inviting to participate?*

I selected people who I believe will benefit from the change. In some cases they will develop new skills that will help them move to the next level. In other cases, it will give them the opportunity to showcase their skills. I do also see some risks. We have a couple of people on the project team who might not be able to stay on the project for the duration based on their personal commitments. I need to make sure we are training people to backfill them, but we do not have anyone who is a great fit for a couple of the key roles and we need people who know the business, so we are building the best team possible. I did validate that all participants on the project team will do a good job while they are on the project. They will be dedicated and make the right decisions for the organization.

■ *Do I believe the people on the teams are being positioned for success?*

The individuals and the teams are positioned for short-term success. We'll need to backfill some key roles while people are on the project team and recruit for some key project roles as the people filling those positions will only play a temporary role.

What do I do?

■ *Who are the right people and how do I place them in charge of the biggest opportunity (not the biggest problem)? How do I recruit them for this personal and business transformation?*

I am recommending some of our strongest players for this project as it will make a huge impact on our business. I also know we need to keep the business running so in some cases, the strongest players will run the business while others go to the project. I have made sure everyone recommended for the project is an "A player."

■ *What am I doing to retain the participants in the company and on the project?*

I will need to pay long-term attention to this. I plan to provide additional mentoring to those who are willing to be part of this important project. I realize that project work is very demanding—much more than the requirements of many of our jobs. People will be asked to do work they are not yet competent at, for example learning new systems and processes. Additionally, many of them will be traveling as part of the project so they will have additional time away from home. Even worse, some of them will be on the project and see their peers who have not made the sacrifices get promoted. I will need to stay aware and also rely on our project team coach to keep me informed about specific issues as they arise so I can address them quickly. I would also like to find opportunities to provide additional development support for project members. That said, I know they will be working long hours, so this may not be the time to offer benefits like employee coaching for some while for others it will be the perfect time. Having a coach as a resource to the project team will make a real difference. This individual will work with key project team members to attend to their professional development goals during this project, as well as team interpersonal and leadership growth goals. The coach is also a sounding board who will help the team through individual and group challenges. The decision to bring in a coach is something I am quite proud of because I am making a resource available to my team that has been a real asset to my own career development. This transition means that we'll need to quickly address conflict and a range of human dynamics—having a coach on staff will support this need.

What do we believe?

◼ *What are the social and cultural norms that dictate who should lead the project?*

Our culture says that we respect the hierarchy. I did that in some cases (with my recommendations), but in others there were really better people to fill these roles. In a couple of other cases, the person who would have been the obvious fit was not the right person because of the importance of his current role, or our inability to backfill the position, or even their inability to work well in a team environment. I needed to consider lots of factors when making selections. I will need to help those involved understand why they were, or were not, selected. In some cases, this decision will spark some necessary job performance discussions.

◼ *Do people leading the change have the right support to change the culture as appropriate?*

As a steering committee we will need to pay attention to the culture. As I mentioned earlier, I think this project will force us as a leadership team to look really closely at our culture and what needs to change. We will do that as a separate activity, not included in the official project plan, but certainly an important activity for us to consider. We may do this as part of our next annual strategic planning retreat.

How do we do this?

■ *Does our hiring strategy support attracting the type of people we are trying to find? Are we asking the right questions in the interview process to select people who can successfully implement change?*

As our culture changes based on what is required to be successful going forward in our industry and also for the project, I believe we will need to look for a slightly different staffing profile. In the past we placed a premium on people who wanted to work for us for their entire career—people who were "steady eddies." Now, I think we need to look for a mix of those steady people and also more people who are comfortable with change and even those who will be consistently looking for ways to improve what we do. I believe that over time we will have more people who are improvement-focused and fewer people who are stability focused. At least if I believe what I have been reading, we will only survive if we make the ability to change one of our core competencies—and, right now, we are not there.

■ *If the transformation is a long one, how are team members rewarded for their effort and risk? What happens if a team member does not thrive in the project environment?*

This project does happen to be a long one and we will need to reward people for their contribution and for their success. Some of those rewards will be with promotions and new roles in the organization as it changes. Some people on the team are actually designing their future jobs through the project activities.

There will definitely be financial rewards given every six months for project involvement. When possible, I would like to connect bonuses to project phases to promote the focus on meeting goals and deliverables. They will be completion bonuses if milestones are met on time and budget.

If a team member does not thrive in the project environment, we need to let him return to his normal job without penalty although he may need to stay on the project until a suitable replacement is identified and in place. There will be cases where employees will not get what they want when they want; we will make decisions for the good of the project and, at the same time, we will look for appropriate ways to acknowledge those employees making sacrifices for the company. These acknowledgments may be financial, but, in most cases, will not be.

Employees who accept the project role and completely fail, or do not perform in a professional manner expose themselves to risk. While it is unfortunate that someone who would take an opportunity to work on a project could actually damage his career, it is also a real possibility. It is the job of the leader and manager to select wisely so that people do not inappropriately expose themselves to risk.

After the selection process, Paul indicated that he was glad he took the time to reflect on his choices as it did impact some of his decisions. Now it is time for you to answer the reflection questions if you are working on a change initiative and at the phase where you are selecting your team. Again, we encourage you to answer the reflection questions along with using the selection criteria to identify the best candidates for the role.

Throughout this chapter we have discussed criteria for team members at various levels within the project as well as provided reflection questions. This should serve as the foundation for you to make decisions on who to include on the team in multiple capacities.

CHAPTER 8

Analyze Situation and Strengths

Fig. 8.1 Innovative Leadership Development Process

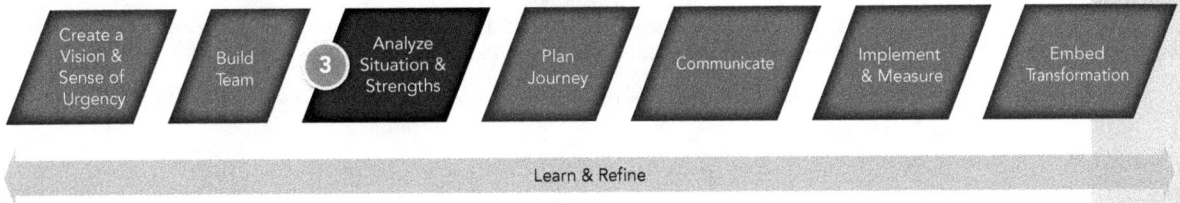

Create a Vision & Sense of Urgency → Build Team → **3 Analyze Situation & Strengths** → Plan Journey → Communicate → Implement & Measure → Embed Transformation

Learn & Refine

Analyze Situation and Strengths

Now that you have begun developing and clarifying your transformation initiative based on the vision, charter, and selection of team members, it is time to collect data that will serve as the foundation for planning activities. The combination of the vision and your understanding and analysis of the current state will give you a solid foundation to determine the gaps between where you are now and where you want to be. This chapter will help you understand the range of assessments you will want to consider in evaluating your current state and change readiness. In a large change project, this phase can take several months.

It is important to combine your vision with a firm understanding of the four key dimensions of your situation to create a complete picture of your current situation. These four dimensions are leader intentions, behaviors, organizational culture, and systems and will be the key components of the transformation effort. This data will help you clarify what needs to change within the organization and what you need to change about yourself to successfully lead the change. The assessments will give you clear information about your current state. This information in conjunction with your vision will help you confirm and refine the project scope.

To ensure assessments are comprehensive, they must capture data from each of the four dimensions. It is important to get a snapshot of transformation readiness in each of the four areas. Many organizations are already using assessment tools that cover several of these areas.

Table 8.1

ASSESSMENT OVERVIEW
Leader Mindset – Am I able to successfully lead a complex change? Does my Type and Developmental Perspective match with the project responsibilities?   ■ Evaluate <u>leader's ability to lead the change</u> – leadership competencies associated with transformation and Developmental Perspective   ■ Evaluate individual attitudes toward the change and <u>willingness</u> - individual change readiness   ■ Evaluate individual <u>ability</u> to change – individual capacity to change   *Recommended tool: Enneagram, MAP Assessment (from Chapter 2), Change Readiness Assessment*
Leader Behavior - How do my actions impact the project success? Do my leadership behaviors align with the project requirements?   ■ Observe how <u>leaders model critical behaviors</u> associated with a successful transformation such as open exploration of issues and alternatives for existing constraints   ■ Observe how leaders <u>create a shared vision</u> across multiple groups within the organization   ■ Observe <u>individual outcomes</u> and their contribution to overall project goals   *Recommended tool: Resilience Assessment and Leadership Circle Profile 360 Assessment*
Organizational Culture - How does our culture support and inhibit the project success?   ■ Evaluate the organization's <u>culture</u> against cultures that support successful transformation and determine the gap using a culture assessment   ■ Identify gaps and opportunities of focus   *Recommended tool: M&A Culture Gap Analysis*

What systems, procedures, and processes do we need to put in place to ensure success?

- Evaluate the project's impact on <u>stakeholders</u> and when to plan communication, training, and job change activities by stakeholder group

- Evaluate business performance using clearly established <u>metrics and process owners</u>

- Evaluate the <u>organizational structure</u> and determine what is necessary to support the desired project outcomes that fit within the future organizational norms

- Conduct <u>Team Effectiveness Assessment</u> to determine process and organizational system changes that would support project success

- Evaluate organization's <u>readiness</u> to adapt to change

- Evaluate the <u>current communication</u> tools and frequency as foundation for project communication plan

- Assess <u>job changes</u> on key roles including task change and workload changes

- Determine <u>risk</u> of the change initiative on the business; identify items such as Day 1 risks as well as project risks

- <u>Technology tools assessment</u> to identify what technological tools you will need to acquire to facilitate the change initiative

- Provide <u>consequences</u> for performance

Recommended tools:
- *Stakeholder Impact Assessment*
- *User Impact Analysis*
- *Existing Business Scorecard*
- *Team Effectiveness Assessment*
- *Change Readiness Assessment*
- *Risk Assessment*
- *Communication Survey*
- *Quality Assessment*
- *Change Readiness Assessment*
- *Technology Tools Assessment*
- *Change History*
- *Change Initiative Inventory*
- *Change Foundation Scorecard*

Assessment Tools

Now that we have presented assessments from the four different dimensions, you will have the opportunity to select those that best meet your needs, then determine how best to use the results. It is important to remember the balance between investing time and money in assessments to ensure you are making sound decisions in line with the expectation of your constituents that you deliver results quickly. We tend to look for opportunities to deliver quick results while time phasing the assessments and building comprehensive plans that will truly support project success. An important element is how assessments provide an early opportunity to engage multiple stakeholders, to understand their perspectives, and begin building support for the project. People tend to commit to projects when their opinion is sought in ways that respect their time and expertise.

We will start with leader assessments then move to culture and organizational assessments. As a reminder: ***If leaders are trying to implement changes that are adaptive (complex changes that require the leaders to change themselves in the process of changing the organization), they will sub-optimize the project outcome if they are not personally growing and adapting.*** Because project changes often require that leaders step into new ways of thinking and new roles, it is important to assess them as the foundation for leader development and coaching as part of the overall project plan.

It is important to note that how others perceive you is based, in part, on their own values and overall view of the world. Interpreting assessment data, particularly input from others, can be just as much an art as it is science. Rather than taking such feedback at face value, we suggest trying to understand the stance of those evaluations, as well as the culture of the organization. Generally, the data and feedback are the beginning of an analytical process for leaders to determine what changes are most aligned with your goals and those of the organization.

For example, if someone is very results oriented in a culture that prefers collaboration, that individual may be perceived as having a negative disposition: controlling, driven, and autocratic. Alternatively, another organization with a different culture more aligned with a results-driven approach may perceive that very same individual as being extremely positive: achieves results, vision-focused, and system-oriented. Part of understanding development and effectiveness is finding an organization that aligns with your leadership style, as well as a culture that can support your potential to grow.

It is very helpful to take multiple assessments at the same time to paint a more complete and accurate picture of who you are as a leader. For example, the Enneagram shows your personality type; the MAP shows your ability to take multiple perspectives associated with levels of development; and the TLCP shows how you are perceived by others as well as how you see yourself. This combined or integrated assessment allows you to better understand your innate skills and abilities as well as your opportunities and this comprehensive information allows you to determine how you can best support the transformation effort. Keep in mind that interpreting the data from these and other assessments requires specialized expertise and we strongly recommend working with a certified coach. Similar to getting medical tests, the potential value of the information is only realized with proper translation. To that end, having a coach interpret the series of assessments as the foundation for your development plan and organizational role can significantly increase your results since you will know exactly where to focus your efforts.

There are several good assessments available. We have used these suggested tools extensively with our clients and recommend them with a high degree of confidence. Moreover, we find that each tool provides vital information in helping to convey a comprehensive picture of strengths, weaknesses, and opportunities. These assessments are aligned with the five key components of Innovative Leadership discussed in Section I of the book. There are many highly reliable and effective tools beyond what we suggest, and we recommend that you explore additional tools that feel right to you.

We will now review a subset of the tools provided in Table 8.1 – Assessment Overview.

Leader Mindset – Type and Developmental Perspectives significantly influence how you see your role and function in the workplace, how you interact with other people, and how you solve problems. The term "Developmental Perspective" can be described as "meaning making," or how you make meaning or sense of experiences. This is important because the algorithm you use to make sense of the world influences your thoughts and actions. Incorporating these perspectives as part of your inner exploration is critical to shaping innovative leadership.

The primary reason for leadership development is that it significantly impacts an organization's ability to successfully implement a business transformation, and the associated process and cultural transformation.

According to Rooke and Torbert in separate articles:

> *"In ten longitudinal organizational development efforts, the five CEOs measuring at the late Strategist/Leader stage (Level 5 Leaders) of development supported 15 progressive organizational transformations. By contrast, the five CEOs measuring at pre-Strategist stages (levels below Level 5) of development supported a total of 0 progressive organizational transformations (no change in two organizations; a three stage regression in one organization; and three stages of progressive development in two organizations). The progressively transforming organizations became industry leaders on a number of business indexes. The three organizations that did not progress developmentally lost personnel, industry standing, and money as well."*
>
> *—Organization Development Journal*

> *"Only the final 15% of managers in the sample showed the consistent capability to innovate and successfully transform their organizations."*
>
> *—Harvard Business Review*

■ **Leader Type Assessment Using the Enneagram.** We recommend using the Enneagram first and foremost to <u>discover your own personality type</u> and (where possible) to ascertain the types of those with whom you are interacting. The Enneagram is used for personal growth, relationships, therapy, or in the business world as an indicator of an individual's primary personality type. As you read in Section I, having an accurate understanding of type can be very helpful. The *<u>Riso-Hudson Enneagram Type Indicator</u>* (version 2.5) provides a reliable, <u>independently scientifically validated</u> tool for that purpose. Please remember that discovering your type is only the first step in the process of self-discovery and working with this system. Finding your type is not the goal, but merely the starting place for a fascinating and rewarding journey of self-reflection.

The Enneagram helps you see your own personality dynamics more clearly. Once you are aware of the importance of personality types, you see that your own style will not be equally effective with everyone. Thus, one of the most useful lessons of the Enneagram is how to move from a style of interacting in which others are expected to mold themselves to your way of thinking and values, to a more flexible style in which you act from an awareness of the strengths and potential contributions of others. By doing so, you help others become more effective themselves—and, as a result, harmony, productivity, and satisfaction are likely to increase. (Source: www.enneagraminstitute.com/practical.asp). The Enneagram report is a text-based report that provides the leader's score for each type since leaders' results will encompass some of each type with one or more dominant types.

- **Developmental Perspective** – Here we recommend using the Maturity Assessment Profile (MAP) to evaluate Developmental Perspective. Susanne Cook-Greuter developed this assessment to describe Developmental Perspectives as part of her doctoral studies at Harvard University. This is widely considered one of the most rigorously validated, reliable, and advanced assessment tools to evaluate adult leadership development. Participants taking the assessment complete thirty-six sentence stems (e.g., When someone needs help…?). The freeform response format allows test takers to give a broad range of information that provides the scorer with ample data with which to evaluate varying developmental features along three main lines: cognitive complexity, emotional affect, and behavioral/action logic. Action logic is how people tend to reason and respond to life. It is critical for the test subject to be completely open and honest when taking this assessment in order for the scorer to have sufficient data to provide an accurate score. We have included sample feedback below to illustrate the leader's results across a bell shaped curve.

Fig. 8.1 Sample Feedback from the MAP

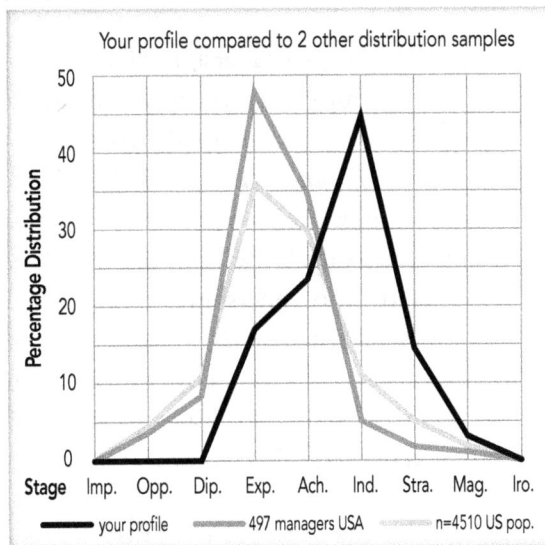

Stage	Distribution of 36 responses by sentence #
Impulsive	-
Opportunist	-
Diplomat	-
Expert	17, 23, 29, 32, 34, 35
Achiever	6, 9, 11, 18, 21, 24, 26, 27
Individual	1, 2, 3, 5, 7, 8, 12, 13, 15, 20, 22, 25, 28, 31, 33
Strategist	10, 14, 19, 30, 36
Magician	5
Ironist	-

Your profile compared to 2 other distribution samples

Percentage Distribution

Stage: Imp. Opp. Dip. Exp. Ach. Ind. Stra. Mag. Iro.

— your profile   497 managers USA   n=4510 US pop.

Leader Behavior – Both Resilience and an assessment of behavioral competencies are helpful to identify a leader development plan to accompany the organizational development plan.

1. <u>Resilience</u> - As a leader, you need to be physically and emotionally healthy to do a good job. In addition to physical and emotional health, the resilient leader also has a clear sense of life purpose and strong supportive relationships. For most people, enhancing Resilience requires a personal change. Our message is that creating and maintaining Resilience is essential to your success. As you improve your Resilience, you will think more clearly and have a greater positive impact in your interactions with others; investing in your Resilience supports the entire organization's effectiveness.

   Metcalf & Associates created a basic tool to help you assess your attitudes and practices that help support Resilience and identify those areas where you can further build your capacity. It is based on fundamental stress management research including the characteristics that support "stress hardiness," a concept pioneered by Kobasa, and research by Gallup and the Human Performance Institute on the Corporate Athlete. (Refer to Section I, Chapter 3 on Resilience for more extensive details. This assessment is available on the Metcalf & Associates web site <u>www.metcalf-associates.com</u>.

2. <u>Leader Behavior</u> – Leadership skills and hard skills are critical to success, and serve as objective performance measures of innovative leadership. Hard skills fall into ***two primary categories: industry-related knowledge, skills and aptitudes***; and ***functional knowledge, skills and aptitudes***. Leadership behaviors are the result of knowledge, skills, and aptitudes specifically related to the craft of leadership. We will use the term "Leadership Behaviors" in this book when referring to leadership knowledge, skills and aptitudes and the resulting behaviors. Both hard skills and leadership behaviors are critical to organizational transformation. The balance between the importance of hard skills and leadership behaviors will shift as the leader progresses in the organization, with leadership skills and behaviors becoming increasingly important with career advancement.

   We use the **Leadership Circle Profile** (LCP) and the associated framework from The Leadership Circle® to explore leadership behaviors. The Leadership Circle Profile is an assessment tool that collects feedback from the leader's boss, boss's boss, peers, and subordinates to provide a 360-degree perspective of the leader's performance along with the leader's self-assessment. The LCP is a unique competency-based assessment and includes belief systems and assumptions that underpin a leader's behavior. This tool integrates well with other tools, such as the Enneagram leadership type model, and MAP, Developmental Perspective model, in a way that provides great insight to leaders.

Fig. 8.2 Sample TLCP Feedback

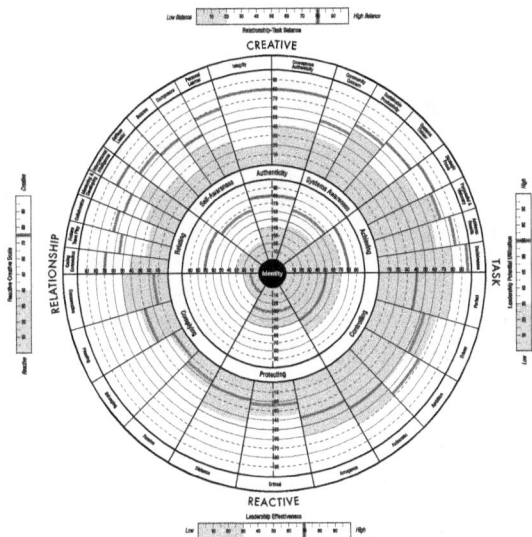

In looking at this simple example of feedback, you will notice that the graph shows high scores in both task creative and task reactive areas (more grey on the right side). From this part of the score we can tell that others perceive this leader as more task-focused than people-focused. This score may be appropriate for the job, or this leader may learn from the assessment that he is not giving enough attention to people-related components of leadership. An additional piece of information is also important. Above the grey shading are lines that reflect how the leader self-scored. This leader sees his behavior differently than peers see him—this difference could be an inaccurate self-perception. It is important that leaders have an accurate view of what others see to be able to make appropriate changes and gauge the impact of these changes. This tool not only allows you to identify possible behavioral changes, it can also help you improve your self-awareness, specifically by understanding how others see you. It is this ability to see what others see that will allow you to target your behavioral changes and fine-tune your effectiveness.

In addition to understanding your own leadership behaviors, there is great value in exploring behaviors of the team (steering committee and project team). The LCP assessment results can be combined to create a team profile and can help a leader understand how he behaves compared to the team norms. As the leader of the entire group, you will be able to identify strengths and risks based on the composite behavior. You can also map the team behaviors to the culture and identify disconnects. This information can feed into an individual and a team development plan and process.

163

Organizational culture is measured by asking leaders their views on key organizational indicators. Metcalf & Associates created a culture assessment that looks at twenty organizational measures that capture both elements of business model and the organizational philosophy that serves as the foundation for the culture. This assessment uses a one to five scale for each of the measures to evaluate organizational beliefs (often reflected in organizational behaviors). We work with the leadership team to identify where the organization is now and where they need to be to support implementation success. Table 8.2 is a subset of the elements you would evaluate.

Table 8.2

Vision and strategic direction	Customer service
Growth funding	Quality
Decision making	Bias for improvement
Capacity for change	Standardization
Accountability	Centralization
Technology	Communication
Innovation	Resource alignment

The assessment process involves each leader giving his view of the current state and the goal state of the culture indicators. This process is interesting because of the range of responses leadership teams often provide and it identifies gaps not only between current and goal state, but also the gaps between key leaders within the organization. When assessment results are highly divergent, the assessment process results in facilitated discussions to help leaders begin to come together as a team and create a shared view of where they are going and how they will proceed. This tool can be tailored to specific organizations and is not statistically validated. The purpose of this activity is to create a shared understanding across the team of the current state, future state, and gap to be addressed.

The culture results can also be mapped to the team LCP group scores to identify areas where their observed behavior is not consistent with the culture they are trying to create.

Organization Systems and Processes – This is the area where most change projects focus, looking at the current organization through several lenses (as reflected in Table 8.1). Because entire books are written that provide these tools, we give a few examples of the items listed in the Table. Most organizations taking on major change initiatives either are working with an internal or external consulting firm that has a well-developed assessment methodology. The assessment names and contents vary slightly, but tend to cover approximately the same content.

Stakeholder Impact Analysis

Stakeholders are those who will be directly or indirectly impacted by the change. We will use this information as the basis for additional data collection to define stakeholder expectations as well as a detailed implementation plan. Interviewing stakeholders is your first opportunity to begin engaging them and building commitment to the project. Your goal is more than just gathering information, it is gaining support.

Leaders occasionally overlook the board as they consider stakeholder input. It is important to gather board input for large scale projects that require significant investment. This is another opportunity to build support and excitement for the initiatives you are taking to accomplish the organization's strategy.

Table 8.3

Stakeholder name (Group)	Who to interview	Impact of change	Perception of change	Role supporting change	Level of commitment (h, m, l)

User Impact Analysis

Users are people whose *jobs* will be directly impacted by the change; they are a subset of the stakeholder group and may also be called "change targets" in some change management approaches because they are the ones whose jobs change. We will use this information as the foundation for communication planning, job change discussions, training, coaching plan, and staffing discussions. This assessment is critical to successfully manage human performance risk (the system works, but people do not know how to use it). Again, by engaging users early you begin building support among important constituent groups. This is an opportunity to gather their input and beginning generating support and excitement about the project and their involvement in it.

Table 8.4

Function / process	Process / people changes	New skills	Position changes

Change Initiative Inventory

Most organizations concurrently engage in several change initiatives. To ensure that projects are successful, it is critical that people get clear and consistent messages about changes, how they interconnect, and the impact. Additionally, people have a "change capacity" that gauges how much change we are able to absorb and remain productive. We also have an energy capacity and it is important to manage the amount of energy we expect people to expend. We can go into a deficit zone for a short period of time, but it is not sustainable. If people spend too much time in deficit before a project is implemented, the project implementation could be at risk. By managing the change volume and human energy, you reduce the risk of diverting attention and sub-optimizing project results.

Table 8.5

Change Initiative Inventory				
Change initiative	Description	Who impacted (user groups / plants)	How does it impact project?	Project timing

Document Current Process Flow and Potential Changes

One of the highest impact activities that can happen during the assessment phase is to map the end-to-end process flow for the change. There are several very helpful approaches to mapping process that range from the simple to complex and in some industries there are government standards regulating these process flows. A process flow chart or map indicates from start to finish the steps to successfully accomplish the process. This process flow should include all major process steps organized in "swim lanes," or by job responsibility. Additionally, it should include inputs, outputs, deliverables, and process measures. These process flows can be quite detailed if you are implementing a large-scale change such as an enterprise software implementation. Your project manager will have a clear understanding of what is standard for your industry. As a reference, we provide a sample flow chart of the generic organizational transformation process in the sample section later in the chapter.

After you have documented the current process, identify key areas impacted by the change. This document can help you identify areas with the greatest change and inform how you time-phase the changes.

As an example, for an enterprise software implementation, we discovered that the inside sales team would have the largest volume of job change on Day 1 of implementation as they would be both changing jobs and using a new system for the first time (outside of training and practice time) to respond to customers. Because we identified the change in advance, we actually implemented job changes in advance using a paper version so the day the system went live, the team was only dealing with an automated system for a familiar job. This type of user impact becomes much clearer when you look at a range of assessments together.

It is very helpful to take multiple assessments at the same time to paint a more complete and accurate picture of the broad range of change, the impact it will have on various groups, and also the risks associated with that impact. Keep in mind that interpreting the data from these and other assessments may require specialized expertise. Similar to getting medical tests, the potential value of the information is only realized with proper translation. To that end, having a subject matter expert interpret the series of assessments as the foundation for your development plan can significantly increase your results since you will know exactly where to focus your efforts.

Now that we have presented four different types of assessments, you will have the opportunity to select the ones you are moved to take and consider how best to utilize the results.

Stories and Examples

Our leader, Paul, is a big fan of assessments. He conducted several of them to get a very solid picture of his current leadership capacity as well as that of his key leaders on the steering committee and the project team. Beyond the leader assessments, he also assessed the culture and conducted several assessments on the systems and processes. He will describe his assessment process in the following section.

Leader Individual and Team Assessments

I am an Enneagram Type Three (Achiever) and developmentally a Strategist. I am well positioned to lead or play a significant role on the project. I also asked that the other steering committee members get assessed using the Enneagram and the MAP. I learned that the steering committee Type was also Achiever with a second high score of Challenger. This group is highly focused on initiating activities and getting results. They do not have a high representation from the other process Types called Cooperators or Soloists (these are the Enneagram process types referenced in Chapter 1). This is important information for us to have going forward.

On the Developmental Perspective assessment (MAP), we learned the range is Achiever to Strategist (see Chapter 2 for definition of levels). This is a reasonable range for a leadership team. It will be important for us as leaders to develop working norms that support success for people at all levels. As a team, we will also need to understand that the norms within the steering committee will be different than the norms when collaborating with other people and teams. Many people on the project team will be functioning at the expert Developmental Perspective and will have a very different approach for interaction.

I also encouraged the team to take the LCP and combined the results to look at the collective group. What I learned was that the steering committee is more results-oriented than people-oriented. This orientation made the company very successful in a rather steady state environment. As we embark on a phase where the organization will be implementing significant transformational change, as a steering committee we will need to be very aware of our tendency to prefer results over people. We will need to resist this "habit" and really take the time necessary to coach and mentor people through the many transitions they will face over the next eighteen to twenty-four months.

Culture

To better understand the culture change necessary, the ten person steering committee completed the culture assessment. What we found was that among the group there was a broad range of responses to some of the measures. We worked with a facilitator to better understand our differences and build agreement among our own steering committee with regard to the current situation and what we want going forward. While it took a long time, this was a very helpful exercise for me personally as it helped me understand the broad range of views we have simply on the steering committee. We do not see the world in the same way, so we will need to check our assumptions often. I assumed others would make decisions similar to mine and that is clearly not true. We will need to discuss our decisions much more than I anticipated to ensure that everyone is on the same page throughout the process.

Figure 8.4 indicates the largest gaps in where we are now and where we want to be. The next step is to identify what needs to be addressed and over what timeframe. We determined as a group that our primary needs for the change to be successful are to improve employee capacity to change and resource alignment. Unless these are addressed quickly, the risk associated with the change will be very high. The second high-priority need is communication. Our perception of what is necessary is really out of balance. We will need to continue to look for more effective ways to let people know what to expect throughout the implementation. The scores in this area indicate a lack of understanding of what is necessary.

Systems and Processes

As shown in Figure 8.3, systems and processes generally get all of the attention with regard to assessments, so we will not spend as much time here because this is the area most leaders already have a handle on. One assessment we are including is the User Impact Assessment. It is really important to understand user impact by group as the foundation for implementation planning and, also, hiring, communication, job change discussions, and several other areas.

Fig. 8.3

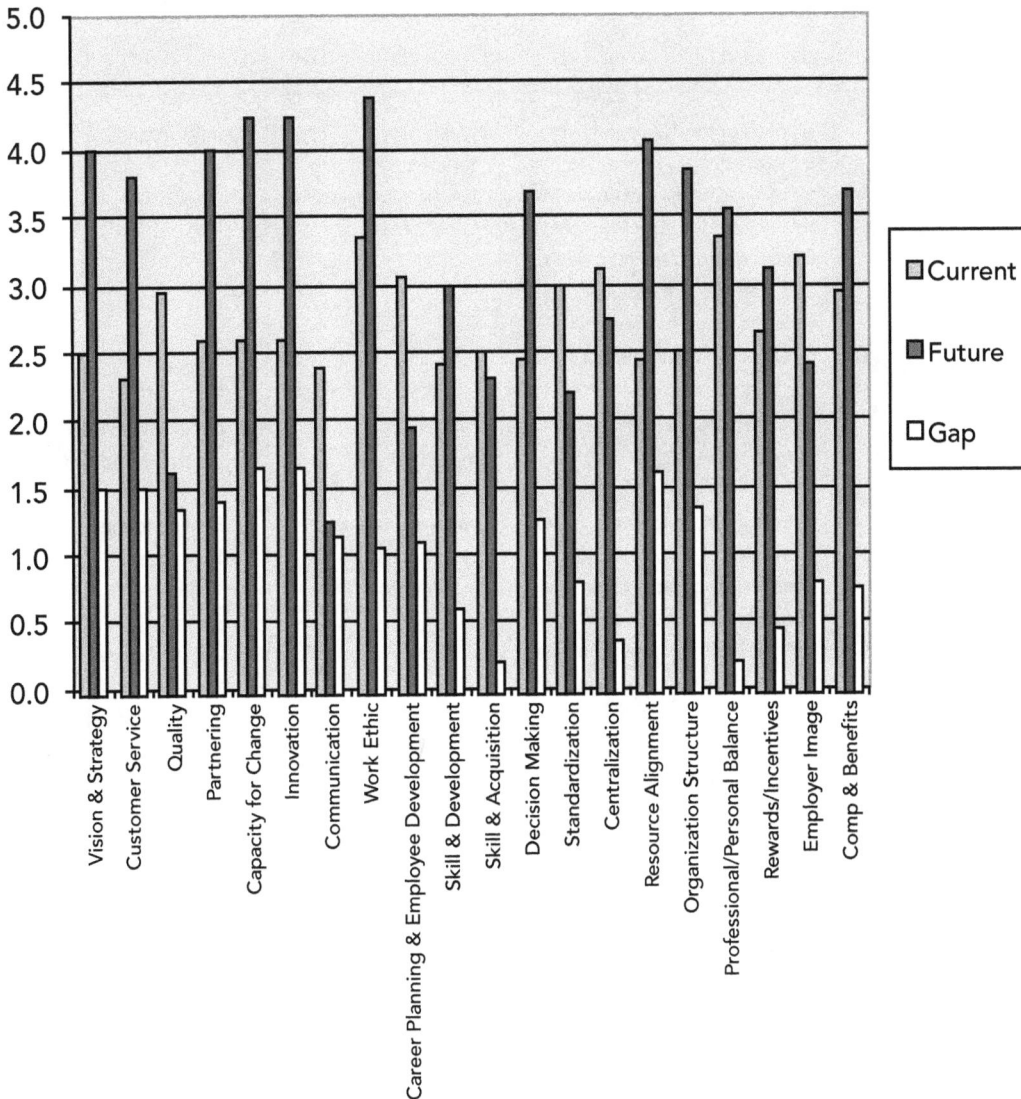

Table 8.6 User Impact Assessment

Function / process	Process / people changes	New skills	Position changes
Sales & Operations Planning (12-18 month time horizon)	An ERP-oriented Sales & Operations Planning (S&OP) process is not currently in place. The work produced by this process will be inputs to the master scheduling process in the system	Conducting an effective S&OP process Important Note: Building S&OP expertise generally takes a minimum of 1-2 years	Master Scheduler Important Note: The Master Scheduler traditionally is the person responsible for orchestrating the S&OP process
Forecasting	All parts of the business must be forecast. New forecasting techniques, tools, and processes will be introduced including best fit forecasting, planning models, and methods to measure forecast variability and bias. Regional managers will own this process	Mastery of forecasting leading practices and system capabilities	Demand Planner
Master Scheduling	1. Process does not formally exist today 2. Use of system tools to manage the overall production plans especially capacity planning to ensure the plans are achievable and provide a high level plan to the schedules 3. Use output from S&OP as input for master scheduling	Mastery of the master scheduling body of knowledge and the use of the system modules (MRP/MPS)	1. Determine role of **Master Scheduler** 2. Role performed by a current employee 3. Determine how the workload and staffing models change
Planner	1. No formal planner role exists today. This is a combination of tasks performed by planning, inside sales, outside sales, and scheduling	ERP skills	

Item Management	1. Currently done within purchasing and inside sales; new function will require significantly increased ERP interaction 2. Create new items and ERP attributes: a. Establish items b. Establish primary and alternate bills of material c. Establish primary and alternate routings d. In the computer system assign the item to the organization that produces it (using codes within the system assigned to each part of the organization)	1. ERP skills 2. Strong company content knowledge	Hire additional people or transfer from existing positions and backfill their roles

In addition to user impact, the most important analysis we did was create the end-to-end process flow. We used it in several different ways. We color coded the chart to identify major risk areas and this information played a large role in our time-phasing of the actual implementation process. We decided to make process changes several months before the system changes. We kicked off an entire initiative to improve several key processes to minimize the impact of the system change, and to accelerate the benefits and change employee habits. If they have developed habits that support system usage, then the probability of errors on Day 1 of launch drops dramatically.

The Organizational Transformation Model in Figure 8.4 was used extensively by the teams because they clarify how they actually do the work. Just like the health check, by putting information on paper, the team members begin to realize they all perform tasks differently and in some cases have very different views on what would be most efficient going forward. By creating and using these process flows, team members develop a shared understanding of both current and future state.

This flow will ultimately be used in training, defining new measures, and overall communications along with the uses referenced above.

Because of the size of the combined charts (12 foot long wall chart with 9 point font) it is not included in this document. We did, however, provide the process chart we used for transforming organizations. This is not organized by role of person performing the task, but rather by major activity to be performed over time. We realize this image is small—it is included as an example, not as your guide. You will create your own process flows based on your specific implementation that could include such items as: roles of people performing tasks, deliverables, hand offs, measures, and risks.

The data we collected during this phase was used to update prior documents such as the change foundation document and even caused slight modifications to the charter. It was also the foundation for several plans we created.

Organizational Transformation Model

Fig. 8.4

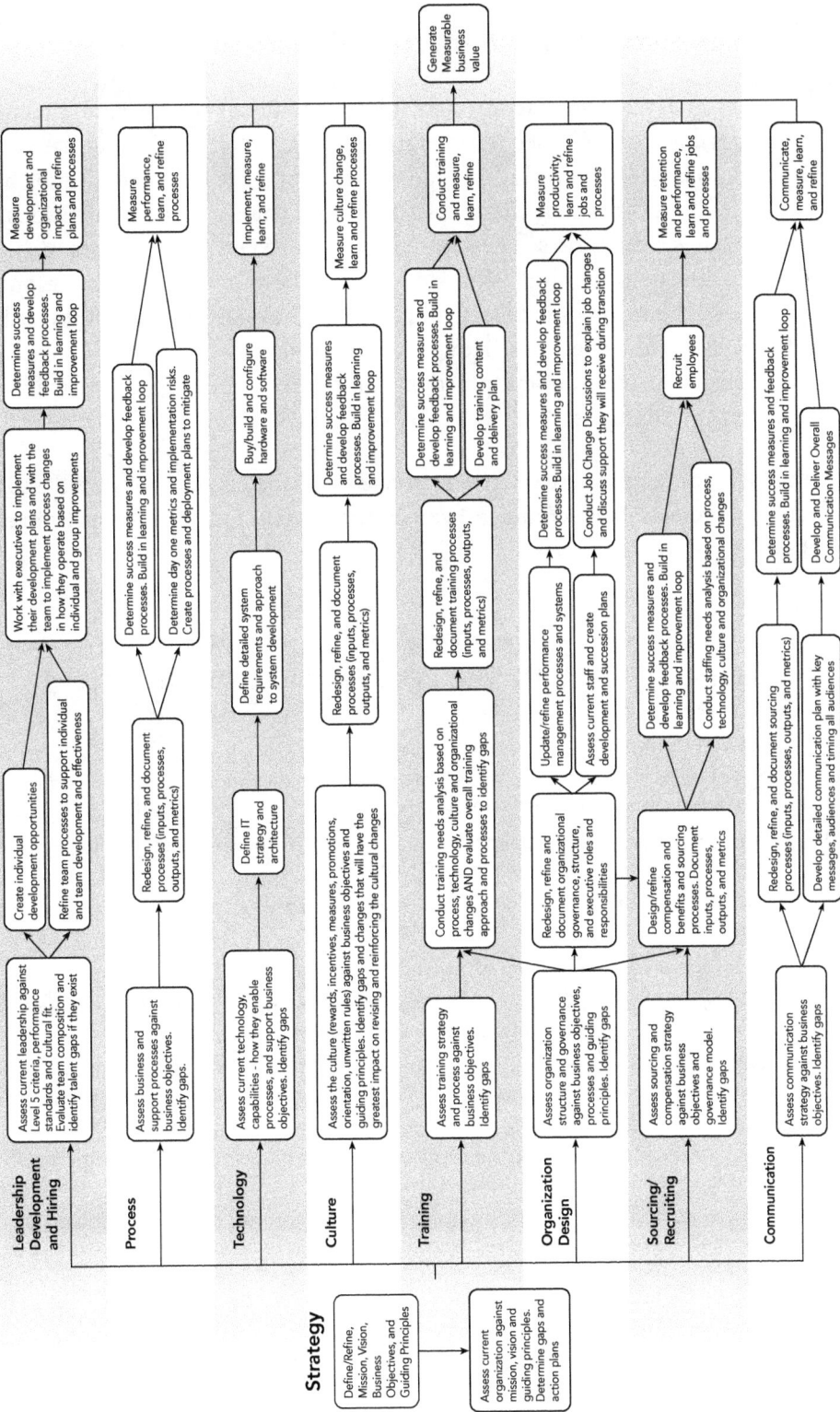

Fig. 8.4

175

Innovative Leadership Reflection Questions

To help you develop your action plan, it is time to further clarify your direction using reflection questions. These questions are organized to reflect the four native domains introduced in Section I and is an opportunity to practice innovative leadership with consideration of how your change plan will affect changes in your intentions, actions, culture, and systems. These questions are arranged to help you explore each of these domains. The questions for "What do I think/believe" reflect your intentions. The questions "What do I do?" reflect your actions. The questions "What do we believe?" reflect culture. The questions "How do we do this?" reflect systems. This exercise was designed to help you start practicing innovative leadership as you analyze your situation and strengths.

The table contains several questions from each domain that are applicable to a broad range of projects. We recommend you **choose two to four questions** from each domain that best apply to your specific situation.

Table 8.7

QUESTIONS TO GUIDE THE LEADER AND ORGANIZATION

What do I think / believe?

- Do I need to change to accomplish my goals? Is the change in perspective or expanded capability at the same level?

- What Developmental Perspective do I think reflects my center of gravity? How will that impact success in my leadership role?

- What level do I think is required for me to perform my job effectively now? In the future?

- How satisfied am I with my performance toward my goals?

- Am I able to balance business and personal commitments? How does my leadership style impact my ability to meet my overall life goals?

- Notice my own interpretation of the urgency of the change and what it means for me personally. What will need to change for me to be the leader I aspire to be?

- How has my leadership style contributed to the organization's success? Have I done things that did not produce the results I had hoped? How would I change to produce different results?

- How would I like to impact the people who work for me? Have they grown and met their career goals while working for me? What have they contributed to the organization while working for me?

- If I am leading a change initiative, what will I need to change to lead this effort effectively? Will I lead the same way this time, or will I change from what I did in the past?

What do I do?

- What assessments am I taking to gather objective data about my performance? This could include performance appraisals, developmental assessments, 360° feedback, or informal feedback from multiple sources. What actions will I take based on what I learned from these assessments?

- How do I model appropriate responses to the sense of urgency in personal actions that are true for me while supporting the organizational objectives?

- How do I use the assessment process to begin building involvement, excitement, and commitment for the project?

- How do I balance my desire to gather data with my requirement to deliver results quickly?

- Have I used the data from all key stakeholders, including our board when appropriate?

What do we believe?

- Are we an organization that believes in assessments and collects data?

- Do we use data to make decisions, or do we prefer intuition or "gut feel"?

- Do we value and trust leadership assessments? Team-oriented assessments?

- Are people willing to share information honestly when you start asking questions about how they do their jobs?

- Are people able to quantify what they do and how they do it?

- Do we understand our current and future culture, and the gaps between?

How do we do this?

- How do we administer the wide range of assessments? Do we have standard tools we would like to use?

- If we collect data for this project, do we want to take time to identify leading indicators to measure going forward, or is this just one-time data collection to help us understand what we need to learn to run the project?

- Can we leverage data we already collect through other means?

- Who will see the data and how will they use it? Are there any concerns that if we share the data it could have an impact on our competitive position?

- What systems and processes are enablers and barriers that will impact my development?

- What processes and measures alert us to urgency in our system that we need to tend to? What are the early warning signs?

- What processes measure your progress? Are you progressing as measured by criteria that will increase your professional effectiveness? Are you progressing against your personal standards? How will your support system or organization reward or punish your changes based on the measures?

- Do the measures indicate a sense of urgency to you that support focusing on development?

Now that Paul has completed the assessments, it is time to take a look at his responses to the reflection questions. He will think through how to use the data he gathered to influence his next steps.

What do I think / believe?

■ *What Developmental Perspective do you think reflects your center of gravity? How will that impact your success in your leadership role?*

During the assessment phase, I learned that I am a Strategist. This developmental perspective will help me play an important role in the success of this project. I also learned that because of my Developmental Perspective, I have different working and communication styles than others. I am coming to realize that I will need to be very deliberate about what and how I communicate with those on the steering committee and even more careful with how I communicate to others outside of the team. I have a tendency to speak over people's heads, or give more information than they want or need from me. It is a tough realization that if I communicate with people the way I want them to communicate with me, I may actually be causing performance problems. This realization really makes me think I need to be more aware.

■ *Are you able to balance business and personal commitments? How does your leadership style impact your ability to meet your overall life goals?*

Because I am an Achiever personality type, I tend to drive myself really hard to succeed. This behavior is nothing new and my family reminds me of it regularly. With the additional responsibility of delivering this project successfully, it will be really important for me to pay attention to my innate tendency to overcommit. If I am not mindful, I will end up exhausted and stressed, and this physical exhaustion will not allow me to behave in a resilient manner when it is most needed. I need to make sure I get time away to refresh my thinking and spend time with my family. It is too easy for me to focus on work and forget about my other priorities in life.

What do I do?

■ *What assessments are you taking to gather objective data about your performance? This could include performance appraisals, developmental assessments, 360° feedback, or informal feedback from multiple sources. What actions will you take based on what you learned from the assessments?*

I took several assessments, the Enneagram for an understanding of my type and the team type, the MAP for Developmental Perspective, and the LCP 360 assessment to see how others view my behavior. Each of these assessments gave me a new way of looking at my own personality and behaviors. As I mentioned earlier, one thing I will take away from all of these assessments is a heightened awareness that I need to take care of myself during this process. I need to pay attention to physical self-care, spend time with family, and get away from work to recharge. One thing I know really helps me is taking walks. I find that I am able to think through complicated problems better while walking than by hours of sitting at my desk.

■ *What messages do you convey that use emotion, external expert sources, and sense of clarity to demonstrate urgency?*

One of the things we discovered as a leadership team was that we are more task-focused than people-focused. We also know that communicating stories is much more effective than giving data. I plan to work with a coach to help me identify the stories that best represent the change we are trying to make and why. I know our product is very helpful to many people yet I still struggle to convey a message that really inspires people so I will get help on this. I watch TED talks (the twenty minute videos) and know that some people are amazing at conveying very complex messages succinctly. I want to be able to do that about our business and succinctly state reasons why this transition is critical.

What do we believe?

■ *Are we an organization that believes in assessments and collects data?*

We are an organization that does not rely heavily on data. We hire good people and they work hard. We have been an industry leader for several years without spending time and money doing things like using dashboards or formal plans. Many people do not even have formal job descriptions. They have not been necessary—everyone just pitches in and gets the work done.

Because many people have worked only at this company, they do not have a history with data collection and this concept will seem strange. Some will really resist it because they will think we do not trust them and that it reflects a disintegration of the "family" culture and moving toward a more corporate infrastructure. We hear these sentiments on occasion when we ask people to make changes.

■ *Are people able to quantify what they do and how they do it?*

If I asked people to estimate how much time they spend on a task, they would have no idea. It is just not how things have been done. I did a small experiment last week where I asked someone how much time he spent on each of his overall tasks and he came back with estimates. The estimates totaled 130 percent. I asked if he was working overtime and the answer was no, it was just that he had picked up the tasks from someone who was out on maternity leave. This is a simple example; you are only working 130 percent if you are working thirty percent more than your standard hours. What I took away from this is that we will really need to help people better understand some basics about measurement—how to calculate and how to use it. I know we will get great value when people just start to identify where they are spending their time and start to make adjustments because of their awareness. I have seen this happen in other organizations and have no reason to believe this will not happen for us also. In many cases, people just being aware of the measures start to improve processes.

This reflection process gives me things to consider as I look at how we develop as an organization going forward and how our culture will impact our success.

Throughout this chapter we have reviewed assessment tools that will allow you to have a strong understanding of your current state, as well as—in many instances—your future state. This information serves as the foundation for a well-planned change initiative. It is important to assess your current state in all of the key domains to identify gaps that will put your project at risk if not addressed.

CHAPTER 9
Plan Journey

Fig. 9.1 Innovative Leadership Development Process

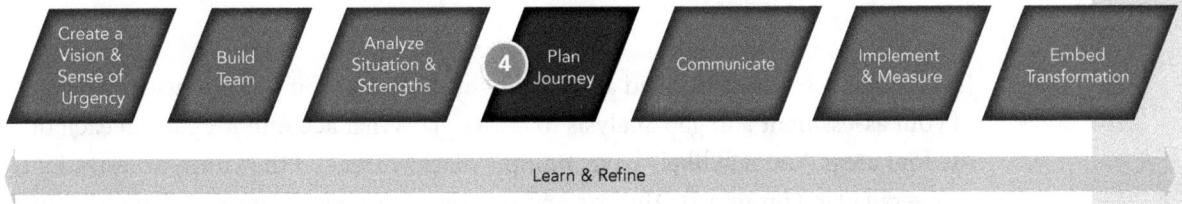

Create a Vision & Sense of Urgency | Build Team | Analyze Situation & Strengths | **4 Plan Journey** | Communicate | Implement & Measure | Embed Transformation

Learn & Refine

This is the stage in which the project team creates the initial plans that will drive the project forward. The role of the leader is generally to clarify the team's expectations and to answer questions, provide input, and review plans. These early plans will establish the foundation for project performance and success. If plans are not thorough, it will be easy to get off track and later realize that course correction is necessary. *A word of caution at this phase: leaders often want to skip, rush through, or minimize this process.* They want to see results and become frustrated at the amount of time and money they are spending on plan development. However, it is often a weak plan that causes a project to fail. One of the six effective tactics in implementing successful transformation is to launch large scale collaborative planning efforts. This collaboration began in the assessment phase when you asked stakeholders at all levels for their input. It will be important to continue to look for opportunities to solicit input on the plan from all groups impacted by the change and, at the same time, do so in a manner that is efficient.

In addition to supporting the planning process at this phase, leaders will be communicating key messages to promote awareness. While the seven step process addresses communication in the next chapter, in reality communication begins during the vision creation phase and continues through the entire project. Leaders will increase team effectiveness during times of uncertainty by sharing personal or team stories of triumph to instill a sense of confidence that the right steps are being taken and that the project will succeed.

As the team creates plans, it will be important to pay attention to how often results are delivered. We previously mentioned the idea of making process changes earlier in the project, implementing software later in the project, and demonstrating progress during the analysis stage. This is important not only to manage the volume of impact on users, but also to keep people motivated. It is tough for project team members to maintain a sense of urgency when they do not have a deliverable for a year or more. By time phasing results and making them visible to the organization, it is easier to engage team members and those who are picking up roles vacated by people who are "temporarily assigned" to the project.

Just as your assessment looked at the four key domains, you will also use the results of your assessment and gap analysis to create plans that account for gaps in each of the four areas. You will likely have multiple plans (projects) that are synthesized into an overall plan (program). The size and complexity of your plans will depend entirely on the size and complexity of the transformation you are trying to implement. Some project plans can be hundreds of pages and highly complex. The templates and samples we provide in this chapter will be much simpler in nature. If you are doing a project that requires very complex implementation plans, we highly recommend you work with people who are trained and certified in project management and have extensive experience.

The table below provides examples of how assessment data can be used as the foundation for specific plans. These individual plans will likely then be consolidated into an overall project plan that is managed by a person or team to track progress, manage task interconnections and interdependencies, identify risks, and manage key decisions and changes.

Table 9.1

TRANSFORMATION ASSESSMENT OVERVIEW

Leader Mindset – Am I able to successfully lead a complex change? Does my Developmental Perspective match with project responsibilities?

- Using the MAP assessment and personality type assessment, identify leader and team development goals. Create development plans

Recommended Tool: MAP Assessment

Leader Behavior – How do my actions impact the project success? Do my leadership behaviors align with project requirements?

- Use results of Resilience assessment and LCP or other 360 assessment and create individual and team development plan

Recommended Tool: Resilience assessment and LCP 360 Assessment

Organizational Culture – How does our culture support or inhibit project success?

Using the Metcalf & Associates (or other) culture assessment current state and future state, identify gaps and create a culture change plan. You can augment this analysis by evaluating LCP 360 results if you use that assessment and have the overall results consolidated

What systems, procedures, and processes do we need to put in place to ensure success?

- Evaluate business performance using clearly established <u>metrics and process owners</u>
- Provide <u>consequences</u> for performance
- Evaluate the <u>organizational structure</u> and determine what is necessary to support the desired project outcomes and fit within future organizational norms
- Conduct <u>Team Effectiveness Assessment</u> to determine process and organizational system changes that will support project success
- Evaluate organization's <u>readiness</u> to adapt to change
- Evaluate <u>current communication</u> tools and frequency as foundation for project communication plan
- Assess <u>job changes</u> on key roles including task change and workload changes
- Determine <u>risk</u> of the change initiative on the business; identify items such as Day 1 risks as well as project risks
- <u>Technology tools assessment</u> to identify what technological tools you will need to acquire to facilitate the change initiative

Recommended Tools –

- *Existing Business Scorecard*
- *Team Effectiveness Assessment*
- *Change Readiness Assessment*
- *Risk Assessment*
- *Communication Survey*
- *Quality Assessment*
- *Change Readiness Assessment*
- *Technology Tools Assessment*
- *Stakeholder Impact*
- *Change History*
- *Change Initiative Inventory*
- *User Impact Assessment*
- *Stakeholder Impact Assessment*
- *Change Foundation Scorecard*

As you review the assessment results you compiled during the assessment phase, it is now time to determine where to take action. You can start with the leader assessments for both individual and team effectiveness. We have provided several templates below that will support your development planning.

For the individual leader, you may want to use the Leader Development Worksheet, Table 9.2, to identify the impact of specific behaviors on individual and team success. We recommend that you present individual and team results, and then ask each leader to consider the top three areas for improvement and complete the worksheet for each of them. Given the time and energy leaders will be spending on the project, the highest priority is to identify any behaviors that will derail the leader, the team, or the project. As Paul mentioned, a tendency to overwork and become exhausted and short-tempered must be addressed as it will have an adverse impact on the project. Part of the goal with the planning process is to identify significant barriers or threats that need to be addressed during the project. Development requires an investment of time and energy. It is important to have a clear understanding of what will be required during the project and how development is included in the investments leaders are making in the project.

Table 9.2

LEADER DEVELOPMENT WORKSHEET – INPUT TO DEVELOPMENT Evaluate and Select Behavioral Change Priorities			
Key Actions	**Detailed Action Planning**	**Skill 1**	**Skill 2**
Select behaviors	Which behaviors do I want to improve or change? Which behaviors do I perform well that I would like to enhance?		
What are the consequences of this behavior?	What will happen if I continue to demonstrate this behavior in the future? How does this behavior impact my customers? How does it impact my career? How are my colleagues impacted? How is my organization impacted?		
Why do I demonstrate this behavior?	I have developed behaviors over the course of my life because they make sense. What has changed that now makes this behavior ineffective?		

How would I like to perform in the future?	Write an end-result statement describing the changes I will make and the impact of those changes. What will an observer see when I have made this change?		
Who will help me change?	Who could I ask to provide me with feedback on how I am doing? Who would be a good mentor?		
What type of support do I want?	Make an agreement with a person you trust about how you would like to support one another in changing behaviors. How will that person hold me accountable for taking this step? How will I support them in changing their behavior? Is there a group that will support me long term?		
What will I do or not do?	What other actions could I take? What am I willing to commit to doing? What am I committed to stopping?		
When will I complete actions?	When will I have completed action items?		

The next template was designed to synthesize development activities reflected in the prior worksheets. Using the information from all of the provided assessments and worksheets, you are now ready to complete your Development Planning Worksheet. This worksheet should reflect the synthesis of your data gathering and personal reflection. This will serve as the foundation for the actions you will take to accomplish your goals. As you define your goals, consider making them SMART goals as defined by the following:

- **Specific** - A specific goal has a much greater chance of being accomplished than a general goal.

- **Measurable** - Establish concrete criteria for measuring progress toward the attainment of each goal you set.

- **Attainable** - When you identify goals that are most important to you, you begin to figure out ways you can make them come true. You develop the attitudes, abilities, skills, and financial capacity to reach them. You begin seeing previously overlooked opportunities to bring yourself closer to the achievement of your goals.

- **Realistic** - To be realistic, a goal must represent an objective toward which you are both willing and able to work toward. A goal can be both high and realistic; you are the only one who can decide the height of your goal; however, be sure that each goal represents substantial progress.

- **Timely** - A goal should be grounded within an approximate timeframe. Goals lacking timeframes also lack urgency.

Table 9.3

DEVELOPMENT PLANNING WORKSHEET				
Current State	Future State / Goal	Actions	By When?	Measure - How do you know?

Now we will take a look at Paul's development plan based on his assessment results. He focuses on his low Resilience scores, and using the Leadership Circle 360 feedback, his behaviors were high on the creative and low on the reactive scales. While his scores were good, he still wants to improve them. He believes these two specific areas will have the most significant impact on the project if not addressed.

DEVELOPMENT PLANNING WORKSHEET — PAUL'S EXAMPLE

Current State	Future State / Goal	Actions	By When?	Measure - How do you know?
Leadership behaviors enhance proactive behaviors (less reactive)	• Increase | effectiveness by modifying my leadership behaviors as defined in LCP assessment. • Clearly spell out vision and build engagement among the team and build on systems thinking (enhance understanding of interconnections of all elements within the system) • Coach and develop staff rather than telling them what to do	1. Modify my behaviors by building team engagement for vision and change agenda 2. Get regular feedback from select team members 3. Evaluate my progress with coach weekly 4. Get involved in key elements of the change process that relate to process mapping to develop a stronger systems awareness within our business and also across businesses in our industry	Focus on these actions for the following year	• Team feedback • Team is growing and requires less intervention • Fewer crises
Lack resilience in the areas of maintaining physical well-being and managing thinking	Maintain health and sense of composure during high stress times	5. Mindfulness based stress reduction 6. Exercise regularly 7. Mental focusing activities	Focus on these actions for the next six months	• Increased sense of overall well-being • Composure under stress • Re-assess using previous metrics

Culture Action Plan

The actions resulting from the culture assessment can be integrated into the overall project plan, or be part of the overall project plan. If the project is large enough to have a centralized project management function, we highly recommend integrating all plans into the central one so task interdependencies and staffing requirements can be identified. The larger and more complex the project, the more important it is to understand all of the activities involved. If you do plan the culture change as a separate document, you may want to use a template like the one included in Table 9.4 that indicates the steps to accomplish, who, when, and measures.

Table 9.4 (Sample)

Guiding Principle	Action - How to accomplish principle	Sub-steps	Who	When	Measure (Specific, measurable, time bound)	Status	Dependencies
Vision & Strategy							
IT executive management solicits input from IT staff concerning vision, long-term direction and priorities before preparing/finalizing the vision and strategies for IT	Create a draft vision statement and incorporate feedback from IT groups before finalizing	1. Facilitate a leadership meeting to complete first draft of vision	Point of contact lead planning sessions with participation of IT Directors	5/19/2012	Draft statement published by 5/23/12	Done	

System and Process Planning

Most large complex projects are run by people with expertise in creating project plans and who are certified using standard tools and processes through organizations like Project Management Institute (PMI). As the leader, it is not likely that you will be deeply involved in creating the plan, but, rather, you will need to have a reasonable level of confidence that the plan—as built—will deliver the outcomes you expect. You will likely be using reports similar to Table 9.5 to track results. These project management spreadsheets or programs may have several thousand tasks, so you may also be reviewing summaries.

In addition to planning the activities to complete the project, it is often important to time phase the project to demonstrate quick wins. If you are using an approach like Agile Development for technology projects, you will automatically have an ongoing release schedule that provides quick wins. If you have not used an agile approach, it is an approach to project management that is typically used in software development. It helps teams respond to the unpredictability of building software through incremental, iterative work cadences, known as sprints.

(Source: www.Agilemethodology.org.) If you are using a more traditional approach, it is important to attend to the timing of results. Following is an example of one of the many approaches to tracking project tasks, level of effort, and progress toward completion.

Table 9.5 (Sample)

Phase - Activity - Task	Units	Description	Days / Unit	Task Effort (Days)	Task Effort (Hrs)	Activity Effort (Days)	Activity Effort (Hours)	Phase Effort (Days)	Phase Effort (Hrs)	% of Effort
1.1 **Establish and Operate the Program Office**								264.5	2116	21%
1.1.1 Management Reporting Processes and Tools						9	72			
1.1.1.a Status Reporting Standards and Format	2	Reports (project & program)	4	8	64					
1.1.1.b Management Reporting Sign Off	1	meeting(s)	1	1	8					
1.1.2 Scope Management/Control Processes and Tools						13.25	106			

In addition to overall project plans, the project will likely have several strategy documents that spell out the approach behind the estimates. The steering committee will likely want to have a clear understanding of the strategy and the associated key decisions that form the foundation of the estimates. You may want to share responsibilities across the team; for example, the HR lead will review communication and training plans while the CIO will review the technology and disaster recovery plans. It will be important to ensure that the various plans coordinate across the group to verify all members of the project team are working in conjunction with one another. You may want to encourage discussions early on with the project team to clarify how they will work together, what they will track, and how often.

If you are on the steering committee, you are responsible for project oversight. You will want to ensure the project team has a plan for project oversight and coordinate with the project team to delineate their roles and yours to ensure proper oversight balanced with granting your team autonomy to accomplish their work. You will want to revisit the charter to ensure that key deliverables and timelines are still correct. You will also want to clarify the level of authority for the project team as well as the level of involvement you want to have. For a large scale change, it is critical that the steering committee is heavily involved (some more than others) as it is ultimately responsible for the overall impact this project will have on the company. Given your overall role in business oversight, you are the most aware of leading indicators and potential risks. Each steering committee will find their own balance for involvement versus autonomy—that will change based on phase of the project, as well as other factors such as project team maturity over time.

As we mentioned at the beginning of this chapter, plans are built on the foundation of work you did in earlier stages. It is important to build on the input you received and continue to gather input from impacted groups on the viability of the plans. Organizations often conduct events such as implementation workshops where they solicit input, prioritize initiatives, identify specific job and role changes, and evaluate risks. This input is then synthesized by members of the project team to ensure that plans are comprehensive, and that participants and stakeholders have been given a voice in the changes that will impact them. This is another opportunity to build commitment early in the change process that pays dividends during implementation.

Innovative Leadership Reflection Questions

To help you develop your action plan, it is time to further clarify your direction using reflection questions. These questions are organized to reflect the four native domains introduced in Section I. As a reminder, this is an opportunity to practice innovative leadership by considering how your change plan will affect changes in your intentions, actions, culture, and systems. These questions are arranged to help you explore each of these domains. The questions for "What do I think/believe?" reflect your intentions. The questions "What do I do?" reflect your actions. The questions "What do we believe?" reflect culture. The questions "How do we do this?" reflect systems. Thus, we designed this exercise to help you start practicing innovative leadership as you create your vision and define your direction.

The table contains several questions for each domain to be applicable to a broad range of projects. We recommend you **choose two to four questions** from each domain that best apply to your specific situation.

Table 9.7

QUESTIONS TO GUIDE THE LEADER AND ORGANIZATION

What do I think / believe?

- Do I need to change my perspective or skills to succeed? If so, what changes are necessary?
- How can I benefit from the success of the project?
- What do I consider my personal short term wins? Project short term wins? Organizational short term wins?
- How do we incorporate short term wins into the project without impacting long term project success, schedule, or cost?

What do I do?

- How can I effectively develop myself and empower others? How do I support their success and the success of the organization?
- What decisions need to be made in the short term to support long-term success?
- What wins can I identify and support that solve "problems" for others, or that are seeds for future shifts?
- How will I deliver clear, concise feedback that will empower others to correct, redirect, or recalibrate their behavior and feel motivated to make necessary changes?
- How do I request and deliver clear and concise feedback that allows me to grow and to support the growth of others?
- How do I determine who is ready for change and what additional support may be required for those who are resistant? Is change readiness included in the plan?
- How am I funding projects and acting to increase organizational awareness and commitment?
- What creative solutions can I find to increase organizational awareness?
- How am I following through on pre-established consequences for behaviors that undermine our success during the planning phase?
- How can I respond to undermining conflicts as learning opportunities?
- How do I encourage bad news, as well as good?
- How am I assigning work to ensure the change is accomplished?
- How am I engaging key constituents to ensure their input is considered and that they are involved throughout the process in meaningful ways?

What do we believe?

- Which wins will provide meaningful results in the eyes of the organization? Which will provide the greatest momentum toward stated organizational objectives?
- Which wins will provide emotionally meaningful results?
- Which stories can we tell about the wins that will be shared with the organization in public settings such as town hall meetings and, also, with our key stakeholders?
- Who are the leaders within the sub-cultures who can best communicate wins?
- Which wins reinforce the changes in our culture and values?

- What is the appropriate reward system based on the organizations values, goals, and culture?
- What are the stories of prior organizational success and do they still support our current project, or do they need to be replaced with new stories?
- How can we connect prior successes to the current change effort?
- Why did we have failures in the past? Have we addressed those issues to ensure they do not happen again?
- Are we building a culture that supports the behavioral traits necessary to support ongoing change such as freedom and empowerment in which employees are free to act within limits to meet their goals?

How do we do this?

- What are the "Top 10" items, in order, we need to get right prior to implementation to succeed? Are these incorporated into the plan?
- How do I build short term wins into the project plan? How do I ensure that early wins are important to key stakeholders?
- How do we track and measure wins and their impact against overall goals? How do we track early warning metrics?
- How do we reinforce and reward behaviors such as developing skills specified in skill building frameworks?
- How do we plan to communicate wins to the larger organization to sustain focus and energy?
- Who do we need to support the change effort for it to be successful? How can our project help key people meet their personal objectives?
- How will we identify short term wins in the context of the larger project objectives?
- How will we connect wins to vision and measures to demonstrate the impact of small steps forward?
- How will we measure (objectively and subjectively) and communicate the merit of wins in relation to overall goals?
- Have we documented all processes and jobs that are changing? Are we following a structured plan to implement the process and job changes across the organization?
- Do we need to provide training to employees or customers to successfully implement change? How much training is required for each group?
- Do we continue to evaluate metrics against stated goals and reinforce success? How do we track a "Top 10" success factor list?
- How are we working with those not accomplishing stated goals to give them the confidence/comfort to take risks, build skills sets, and commit to change?
- What processes need to be enhanced to put the guiding principles into action? Who owns them? How will we implement changes?
- Do the organizational structure and governance approach support the future direction and success of the business?
- What early warning metrics can we create to let us know if we are on track before we have issues (leading indicators)? What metrics do we track daily? Weekly? Monthly?

- How do we convey required new skills using mastery frameworks that spell out detailed skills and competencies for success?
- How will the organization build a reward system that aligns with the new environment to meet multiple motivations (among people or departments)?
- Have we set goals and expectations for each individual that support the overall organization and the change effort?
- What communication processes do we put in place to provide timely feedback? How are stakeholders included in this communication process?
- Have we created evaluation and feedback processes that will be included in the plan to support new behaviors?
- Have we planned to create, communicate, and use processes to identify those not exhibiting or supporting the new strategies and behaviors and understand why this is happening?
- What are we doing to measure, communicate, and fund "learning organization" processes and activities without overbuilding the training?

Now we will see how Paul answered the reflection questions he chose.

What do I think / believe?

- *How can I benefit from the success of the project?*

   I am highly committed to the success of the project as the CIO because it will make my impact on the organization easy to demonstrate. In this role, there is no question about what sales does or what manufacturing does, but running an IT organization can be a continual struggle to show my value. With successful implementation we will increase data security, decrease technology cost, and use technology to enable the entire organization to be more effective. There are still people on the leadership team who do not see how technology can make the overall enterprise more successful.

   I am a leader in the CIO community across the city and it is important to me that I have both a win in my organization and the community. I also want our IT employees to be highly respected across the community and I would like our company to have the best IT talent in town. By having leading edge tools, systems, employee development, and a culture of success, we can attract top people.

■ *How do we incorporate short term wins into the project without impacting long term project success, schedule, or cost?*

As I mentioned earlier, we can implement some parts of the project in phases. We will launch some modules of the software in the first phase along with much of the hardware. This first phase will also include training. I expect that having an early success will decrease the level of resistance throughout the organization. While not everyone will find their job easier, most should see that the organization, as a whole, is more effective and that translates to job security. I think doing the project in phases will actually reduce the cost and have a positive impact on the schedule. Some people will focus on the first implementation and then rejoin the team. This first phase will allow us to test several of our ideas about what will work and what will not. It is through this learning that we will increase the probability of success with minimized impact on business operations.

What do we believe?

■ *What is the "Top 10" list of items we need to get right prior to implementation to succeed? Are these incorporated into the plan?*

I asked our team to create a "Top 10" list as part of the implementation plan and also a list of Day 1 issues—items that need to be addressed in advance to ensure we are successful. After reviewing both lists, I made sure the solutions to them are clearly incorporated into the plan. Additionally, when I look at what the steering committee is tracking, we will be paying close attention to these items to ensure we are proactive in addressing them.

■ *How do I determine who is ready for change and what additional support may be required for those who are resistant? Is change readiness included in the plan?*

We have an entire plan focusing on change readiness. This plan measures items such as: How well is the project being managed; do you trust that leadership is taking us in the right direction; do you have the tools and training to succeed; do you believe this project is good for the company; are you rewarded for implementing the change successfully?

We are measuring all of these items through a survey delivered prior to go live, probably three months for the general population, and again two weeks in advance of going live. We will also use this same tool for the project team on an ongoing basis as an indicator of challenges. The questions may change to fit the exposure and concerns of different groups.

We will use the survey results to determine corrective action where necessary. I will also work through the sponsor group and the extended team to gather feedback from them. One of the steering committee members will be working with both teams and part of that responsibility will be to gather ongoing feedback and identify corrective action.

What do I do?

◼ *How can we connect prior successes to the current change effort?*

We have an organization filled with dedicated, hardworking people. There are lots of stories people recount about how a dedicated employee went above and beyond the job requirements to ensure that a customer was satisfied. These stories trace back to the founder who was a down-to-earth guy who pitched in to get any job done no matter how small. We continue to have a culture that promotes people pitching in to help others across the organization. Since this project will leverage a cross-functional team, that same culture will really support our success. As the CIO, I will look for opportunities to highlight people who accomplish great things.

I also want to make sure we are not rewarding only those people who act heroically. We need people to remember that heroism is unusual behavior and that we really want people to live relatively balanced lives where they work hard while they are here, but they also go home and stay healthy and refreshed so they are thinking clearly while at work. I do not want our organization to run the ERP implementation like others have where the divorce rate of team members goes up and people end up in the hospital for stress-related issues. I have heard lots of stories from other organizations that caution about the negative impact of stress on project team members. I want to make sure the stories we tell will not encourage unhealthy behavior.

- **Why did we have failures in the past? Have we addressed those issues to ensure they do not happen again?**

In the past, each of our business locations functioned autonomously with a separate P&L, so they were not required to implement the common system if they did not want to. If we take that attitude with an ERP, we will have serious issues. Because many of the locations are the result of acquisition, the people running them are the founders. They were willing to sell to us with the understanding that they got to maintain significant control. Those agreements made sense when we ran our organization differently, but they no longer work for us. I know we have a serious communication challenge with some of these location general managers. Buy-in will be more effective than compliance and passive aggressive behavior, and yet, for some, short term compliance may be the best we will get. We do need to make the commitment as an organization that participation is not optional—if you want to remain in the GM role, you will implement the system. We will do all we can to ensure your success.

How do we do this?

- **Who do we need to support the change effort for it to be successful? How can our project help these key people meet their personal objectives?**

This is a really important question and while I do not know the names personally, I know we have chartered a sponsor team and an extended team that will include formal and informal leaders and influencers throughout the organization. I understand it is critical to learn about change not only from the highest levels within the organization, but also from peers and people you trust. By creating a network of people who are trusted, we will create an information channel both ways helping us to identify issues of concern then addressing those issues. I realize these people have full-time responsibilities and this is an additional burden on them. I think we really need to make sure the plans for these teams are well articulated and that they have the tools and information they need to be successful.

- **Have we created evaluation and feedback processes that will be included in the plan to support new behaviors?**

Part of our plan involves review and revision of the performance management process. There are some positions that will need updated job descriptions and possibly a complete overhaul. In some ways these are the easiest to deal with. For positions with significant change, we will create guides that specify what to start doing, i.e. new activities; what to stop doing; and what will continue to be done in the same way as before. We will create these documents as computer-based learning guides. For activities that are beginning, the employee can click on the new task and it will launch a document providing a "quick reference" card that summarizes what the change means. Since people impacted by the change are comfortable using a computer, this seemed like the most effective way for them to learn the new role and also have quick access to detailed information. Since this information will reside on the network, they will have ongoing access as often as they need it. We are aware that some people will quickly adapt to change and others will need these reminders and support tools for a much longer period of time, so we will build a system that supports a broad range of needs.

Others will have minor changes and it will be easy to overlook the updated measures and reinforcement that needs to happen for these.

Now that I have reflected on these questions, I am much clearer about how we will address short-term wins as part of the planning process and I also have a much clearer sense of the range of items that need to be included in the plans. I did not realize how many areas of the organization would be impacted by this system and the volume of work it would require. I guess this is why the planning process takes so long. If we forget a key step, we expose ourselves to risks of which we may not even be aware until it is too late.

This chapter focused on creating a project plan that spells out the actions required for successful project completion as well as the measures to ensure staying on track. The steering committee will be working closely with the project manager to support the team in meeting goals as well as helping to define corrective action when necessary. In addition to creating project plans focused entirely on the change at hand, it is important for leaders to identify areas where their own leadership skills or style may impede progress and plan developmental activities to address these. Project planning generally focuses on the changes that need to happen to systems and processes. This book expands that focus by creating a foundation for leadership development necessary to support project success.

CHAPTER 10

Communicate

Fig. 10.1 Innovative Leadership Development Process

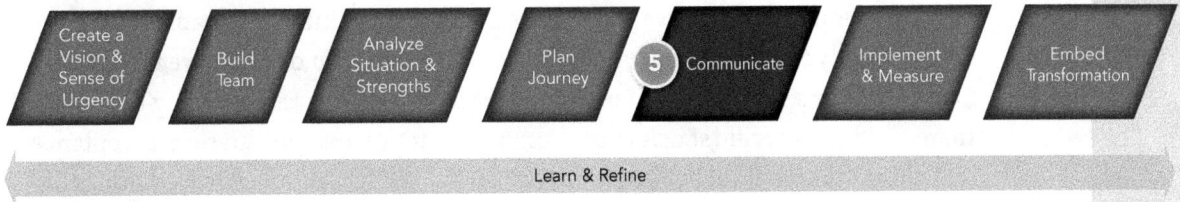

| Create a Vision & Sense of Urgency | Build Team | Analyze Situation & Strengths | Plan Journey | 5 Communicate | Implement & Measure | Embed Transformation |

Learn & Refine

While we have a process step called "communication," as a leader you started communicating as soon as you decided to turn a strategic goal into a project. When you allocated money to the project, you communicated your commitment. When you selected top talent from your organization you were communicating through your actions. If you assigned people who were not perceived as top talent, you were also communicating!

Communication will be broken into phases based on the goal you are trying to accomplish. Initially you want people to be aware of what is happening. Next, you want them to understand why you are making the change and why they will benefit from it. Eventually you will want them to believe in the change and take action (support the change). Different audiences will be getting information at different times throughout the project. As you might imagine, the project team will need to go through the communication to the acceptance phase pretty quickly because you want them to accept a role on the project team. End-users of the system may not need to act until you invite them to a training class eighteen months after the project starts. You will want them to be aware something is happening and you want them to stay focused on their jobs until it is time for them to get involved. ***Messages and timing must be designed to help people understand and respond appropriately.***

Your assessment and planning team should have evaluated the needs of multiple stakeholder groups and built a communication strategy and detailed plan summarizing audience, key messages, and vehicle used to deliver the information. This plan will then be broken into much greater detail to create an actual message map that a communication lead will manage. These messages should be time phased to address the varying timing of each audience. As an example, if you have broken the implementation into phases by location, each location will begin getting these messages based on the timing of their project launch, also known as "go live" for many projects.

Communication supports organizational change by helping employees move up the Change Commitment Curve (see Figure 10.2) which ultimately enables them to act differently to drive organizational success. The version of the curve is based on Daryl Connor's 1992 book, *Managing at the Speed of Change*. According to Connor, there are three specific stages in the commitment process: preparation, acceptance, and commitment. Effective communication is critical in moving people along this curve from initial information about the change to internalizing the change. There have been several variations on this curve over the years; we reference this as the foundation for change commitment discussions because we have not seen anything more effective in discussing how people's commitment to change evolves with time and understanding.

Fig. 10.2

Change Commitment Curve

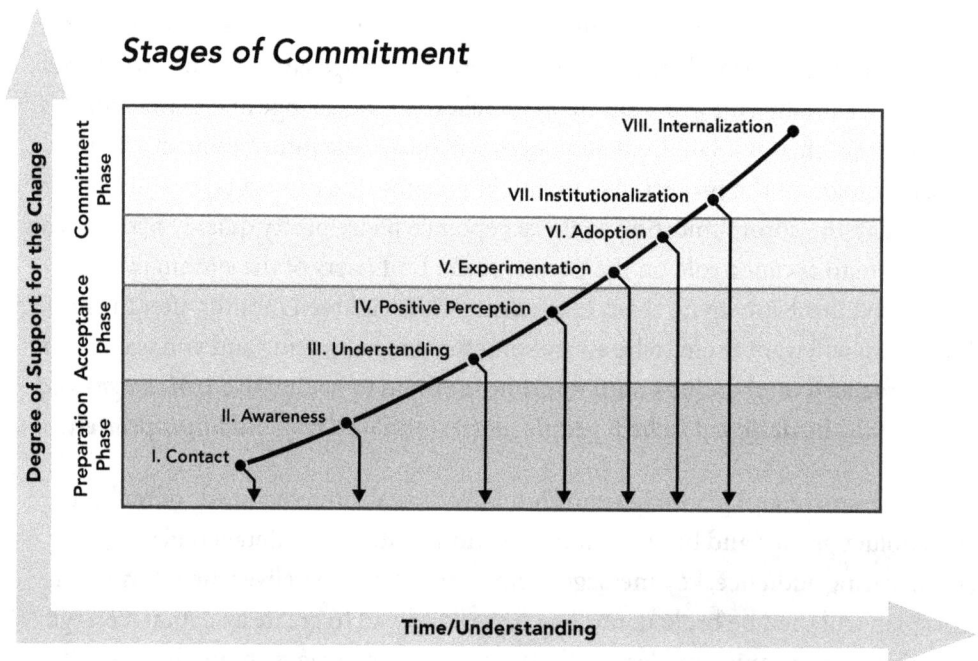

Preparation Phase: The goal of this phase is to have successful contact with the people impacted by the change such that they become aware that a change effort is underway

Acceptance Phase: The goal of this phase is to have those impacted by the change develop an understanding of what is involved in the change effort and believe that this change will be positive

Commitment Phase: The goal of this phase is to experiment with the change is to allow people to test solutions and prove that they deliver value to the organization. As solutions prove effective, people can commit to a long-term integration into the organization

Effective communication is achieved through informing, creating understanding and positive perception, and inviting participation to help achieve buy-in from individuals who will be impacted. It is important at each stage of the change commitment curve that communication is consistent, continuous, and two-way. Specific communication vehicles and messages provide impacted stakeholders with the information necessary to move along the change curve from initial contact to adoption. In addition to the written and verbal messages you send, your behavior must be consistent with what you say.

Many approaches emphasize the importance of "creating a burning platform" at this point. More recent research, including the McKinsey study in 2009 (referenced at the beginning of the book), talks about the importance of implementing an equal mix of positive and negative communication. We have a bias toward an approach using both positive vision and negative consequences if the vision is not successfully implemented. You will decide the right mix depending on your situation and culture.

The Communication Plan is designed to guide the project communication effort. It is generally divided into five parts:

1) **communication strategy:** the high level description of our approach to conveying messages;

2) **detailed action plan:** indicating specifically who will communicate which messages to which groups and the expected outcome of each communication event;

3) **measurement and tracking plan:** describes how we will track communication effectiveness including sample assessments;

4) **data collection plan:** drives our approach such as the audience analysis; and

5) **templates:** for many of the communication vehicles and forms to be used in the communication process.

A standard approach considers the elements of message, media, behaviors, and feedback. You will communicate clear and compelling answers to the questions that are uppermost in people's minds. You will strategically choose media so as to enhance the clarity and the impact of the message. Communication will come in the form of face-to-face, small group meetings, road-shows and presentations, general publications for broad circulation, and focused publications for targeted circulation. These messages will be delivered via multiple sources and forums, involving executives, organizational leaders, project team members, change network members, and others involved in the change. Over the period of the implementation, locations that have successfully implemented the change may also be involved in communicating their process for change and the successes they have accomplished.

Fig. 10.3

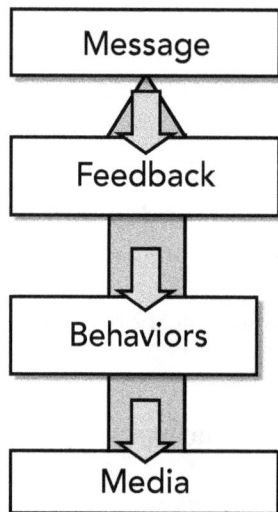

The most important factor is active involvement by executives, including the CEO for high visibility projects, and members of the project team, implementation teams, and, if you have one, the extended team or change network. Without active involvement of teams and leaders, the communication effort will be unable to achieve its objectives. Communication cannot be delegated—it is the responsibility of the leaders.

The question we get most often during change is, how much and how often do I need to communicate? The thing to remember is that you convey the information every time you speak to a broad audience of people during the day. Each person may only hear the message once per month even though you are repeating it continually. According to John Kotter in his January 2007 *Harvard Business Review* article, "Leading Change: Why Transformation Efforts Fail," one issue with change efforts is that vision is under communicated by a factor of ten. His studies indicate, "Executives who communicate well incorporate messages into their hour-by-hour activities. In a routine discussion about a business problem, they talk about how proposed solutions fit (or don't fit) into the bigger picture."

Tools

Paul knows that ineffective communication can jeopardize an otherwise healthy and well-planned change. The following section provides examples of Paul's communication documents. During the assessment and planning phase, the communication lead created a communication strategy and plan. We have included some excerpts below. This approach is based on the model of cascading messages throughout the organization to build support and create a demand for the change.

Communication Objectives – The objectives of the communication effort for the project are to:

- Move everyone who needs to change along the commitment curve according to the project implementation time schedule
- Provide accurate information that will reduce productivity dips associated with lack of information or rumors
- Help individuals prepare for, understand, and accept changes in their jobs
- Inform and involve all impacted groups whose commitment is needed
- Enlist the help of all project team members with the communication efforts
- Build realistic expectations regarding process changes and project benefits and impact
- Provide timely information, appropriately tailored for a variety of audiences
- Sustain interest and energy of project team members and implementation team members
- Maintain high visibility (mind share) with executives who face severe time constraints and maintain a very high level of commitment to the project's success
- Create an image of project as a vital component of the overall organization strategy

Critical Success Factors – The critical success factors driving this communication effort are:

- Maintain top level commitment to the project at the executive and business unit leadership levels, especially in projects longer than three to six months
- Capture all audiences, whether directly impacted or not
- Communicate targeted relevant information in a timely manner
- Leverage process teams for communication and message development as appropriate
- Communicate consistent messages
- Ensure information is accurate
- Solicit feedback and evaluation for continuous improvement
- Ensure communication is coordinated with other change efforts and activities
- Eliminate overlap or inconsistencies across communication channels

The communication plan will contain a detailed action plan that specifies leader communication goals by project phase. We have included a sample below to illustrate what the leader communication format may be during the early phase of a transformation project.

Table 10.1

COMMUNICATION APPROACH			
Audience	**Info Exchanged**	**Vehicle**	**Frequency**
Executives			
Steering Committee	▪ ERP Education ▪ Status ▪ Issues ▪ Overall progress ▪ Ongoing leadership activities and involvement	▪ ERP training sessions ▪ Steering committee meetings ▪ Leader communication discussions with change management	Bi-weekly Bi-weekly Bi-weekly

Top Executives (Direct reports to VPs)	◾ ERP Education ◾ What do I need to change before Day 1? ◾ Discussions of process and behavioral change? ◾ Change management support ◾ Coaching support ◾ What the impact is on the business strategy and the overall approach to how we do business ◾ Ongoing repetition of why we are doing the project in the first place, including benefits and specific progress toward realizing those benefits	◾ ERP training sessions Top executive meetings – use existing meeting structure to share project status, gain input and begin process and behavioral changes	Bi-weekly (for local people) Use currently scheduled meetings (monthly or quarterly)
Department Managers	◾ ERP Education ◾ What do I need to change before Day 1? ◾ Discussions of process and behavioral change ◾ Change management support ◾ Coaching support ◾ What impact this is having on the business in the mid-term ◾ Resource requirements ◾ What I need to do to facilitate implementation ◾ Ongoing repetition of why we are doing the project in the first place, including benefits and specific progress toward realizing those benefits	◾ ERP training sessions - video ◾ Meetings ◾ Newsflash ◾ Implementation workshop	TBD TBD Bi-weekly TBD

One of the tools many leaders use to communicate is ongoing talking points. Our communication lead will prepare these for us monthly and it is our job to make sure we are communicating these points at every possible opportunity again based on the communication plan and timing.

Leader Talking Points - Objective: This activity is designed to increase focus on key messages. These messages will be tailored to different audiences and will change as we move through the change process. Initially we will be focused on clarifying the vision and creating a sense of urgency, and reinforcing to the team that their contribution is valued and that they will be rewarded after the project with positions that take into account their new skills.

Table 10.2

MUSCLE MEMORY / THEME FOR THE MONTH		
■ **Old:** We have good people working hard. They will do the right thing and we will be profitable ■ **New:** We have good people working hard. With clearly defined standard processes, process owners, metrics, and effective ERP usage, they will have the information and discipline to do better things and we will be more competitive and/or profitable		
Target Audience	**Questions to Ask**	**Messages to Convey**
This Week		
Process owners and project team members	■ Process owner president encouraged to ask any and/or all of the following questions: ■ All VPs - What process changes are you looking at? ■ Purchasing - to the purchasing managers regarding 80/20 inventory analysis – what is happening with the roll-out? ■ Purchasing - what is the trend in PO due date adherence	■ I am interested in what you are doing and I would like to learn more about how you are using the system and the value it is adding to our business

This Month		
Project team – communicate an understanding of their career concerns	What career concerns do your people have?	**President & VPs** We understand that while you are working on the project your peers are progressing in their functional area, we value the broader business and IT skills you are developing and we will create opportunities for you when you complete the project that will leverage your new skills
This Quarter		
Broad audience - Location monthly discussions - Regional manager meetings - Territory manager meetings - Plant managers - Functional managers	What level of understanding do people have about the system?	**Who:** President deliver & VPs reinforce and customize **What:** Level setting and creating a sense of urgency - - What is ERP - Business trends - Why ERP helps us address the trends

Innovative Leadership Reflection Questions

To help you develop your communication plan, it is time to further clarify your direction using reflection questions. These questions are organized to reflect the four domains introduced in Section I. As a reminder, this is an opportunity to practice innovative leadership by considering how your communication plan will affect changes in your intentions, actions, culture, and systems. The questions are arranged to help you explore each of these domains. The questions for "What do I think/believe?" reflect your intentions. The "What do I do?" questions reflect your actions.

The "What do we believe?" questions reflect culture. The "How do we do this?" questions reflect systems. This exercise is designed to help you practice innovative leadership as you create your vision and define your direction.

The table contains several questions for each domain to be applicable to a broad range of projects. We recommend you **choose two to four questions** from each domain that best apply to your specific situation.

Table 10.3

QUESTIONS TO GUIDE THE LEADER AND ORGANIZATION FOR COMMUNICATING TO MAINTAIN TOP LEADERSHIP LEVEL COMMITMENT

What do I think / believe?

- What do I need to communicate to others about my personal change goals? How do I solicit their input and support?
- What personal stories (actions and emotions) will convey my commitment to the change in a sincere manner and empower others to act?
- How much information do I think is appropriate to communicate?
- Am I willing to dedicate a significant amount of my time to communication?

What do I do?

- How do I show my conviction through my actions ("walk my talk")?
- How do I convey my request for input and support when I fall short of my stated goals at points along the way?
- How do I convey that although I understand others will make mistakes in the process, my expectation is that they will make a strong effort to change?
- How do I tailor and deliver messages to different segments of the organization that inclusively motivate everyone to accomplish the vision?
- How do I convey messages that will make strong statements using both the languages of feelings and of logic to appeal to multiple groups?
- How do I demonstrate humility and give credit to others?
- How do I communicate the vision in a manner that is hard hitting and realistic, yet conveys our confidence that the vision is achievable?
- How do I communicate progress, new challenges, and my support for all that is being done?
- Am I balancing communication messages to include both vision for the future and consequence if we do not change?
- How do I communicate the facts and my hope for the future?
- How do I communicate that the balance between challenge and overload is important and that I want to maintain balance between the two?
- How do I communicate my need and desire for accurate feedback?
- What do I communicate when situations and priorities change?

What do we believe?

- What are our beliefs about communication with regard to who does the communicating? How much information and how often do they share? Do we solicit input or just convey information?
- What is the appropriate language and message content based on the values, goals, language, and culture of each audience segment (department)?
- What type of feedback will we seek from segments to determine if they are buying into the vision (objective and subjective)?

How do we do this?

- Do we all have a good understanding of the communication strategy and our role within that strategy?
- What is our structured communication plan? Who receives communication? When? Through what channel? From whom? What are the key messages? How do we keep multiple audiences informed with the right amount of information at the right time to enhance buy-in and influence behavioral change?
- Do we have any applicable stories connected with company folklore?
- Do people understand that we need to use the rule of thumb "communicate 7 x 7 or 49" for people to internalize the messages? How do we make this expectation the norm?
- Of our current communication methods and vehicles, what will most effectively convey our messages?
- Can we combine and/or eliminate any current communications?
- Would communication be more effective if multiple projects were discussed in a joint vehicle to help the audience better understand the link and impact?
- How do we communicate measures and rewards for successfully accomplishing the vision (ensure a clear link between vision and rewards)?
- What are we currently communicating that should stop because they are not consistent with our vision?
- How do we measure the impact our communication has on buy-in and change?
- How do we improve our communication based on what we learn from measurement?

What do I think / believe?

- **What do I need to communicate to others about my personal change goals? How do I solicit their input and support?**

  I realize that part of communication success is being authentic and making the message personal, and I also realize that this really is not my style. I would feel much more comfortable focusing communication on the company. I think I will talk about how I want to change the reputation in our company so that IT roles are highly sought after and how this will really improve the marketability of everyone on the team (not that we want them to leave). It will also mean we can attract top talent to our team, resulting in high caliber colleagues.

I am comfortable asking that people do their jobs—that is, after all, why we pay them. Can I ask them to go above the call for me? This is tough. I realize people generally make sacrifices for people, not companies, and yet I will only ask them to make sacrifices if I think it is necessary. I will also try to make sure we "restore the balance." By that, I mean if I ask you to make a sacrifice for me, I will want to make sure the company also does something for you so you do not feel manipulated and resentful afterward.

I feel comfortable asking for input if it is in an area in which someone has expertise. I am very careful to make sure I am not asking people what they think in areas outside of their area of responsibility as this tends to increase their insecurity when they wonder why I am asking them about something I should already know and about which they are less knowledgeable. I realize this is another area that requires attention to the nuances. I want to get input, but only on things that make sense. I am certainly not running around asking for input on things I have no intention of acting on—I have seen that behavior end in disaster.

■ *Am I willing to dedicate a significant amount of my time to communication?*

Yes. I am willing to do what I need to do to make the project successful. I am also aware that the period of time over which I must communicate could take much longer than I really want it to and I will need to make sure I do not get frustrated by the process. I know I expect people to "get it" quickly—and some people may not get it and others will resist the changes. Both of those possible scenarios will frustrate me. I know I can manage it if I keep reminding myself that the communication role is really critical and that the message needs to come from me, the CIO. This is a task I cannot delegate to others. I will make an agreement with our communication lead that we talk monthly, and he will make sure I am on track and also give me feedback about the overall communication activities, including successes and opportunities for improvement.

What do I do?

■ *How do I communicate my need and desire for accurate feedback?*

This whole set of communication questions seems to be getting at the same point, I need to be open with others about what is changing and why, and include my own personal struggles regarding the change while still showing that I remain fully committed to it. Well, as an introvert, that does not sound easy for me.

Accurate feedback seems like an easy request. My direct team is already expected to give me the real story on a regular basis. I want an answer based in reality, not fantasy. I will need to set clear expectations with the project team that we, as a steering committee and I, as the CIO, need to know what is really going on and how we can participate. If it means you need to tell me I am the problem, I need to know that. The project success is really important to me and I am certainly experienced at hearing bad news on projects. I expect bumps and issues. We actually have a whole process for tracking risks and issues so we know they will happen. So, this sounds like I just need to reinforce the importance of ongoing candid feedback.

■ *What do I communicate when situations and priorities change?*

As I mentioned above, projects have issues and priorities change. While I realize these changes can be really frustrating, I also recognize they are a fact of project work. Part of what I need to do is communicate just that: priorities will change and we need to address them. We certainly need to make sure they are not changing in an irrational way because we are not managing the project well. After that, we need to realize it is just part of the job. If we want steady workload and predictable processes, we are in the wrong place. If we like the variety and find fixing problems and changing priorities stimulating, then game on!

What do we believe?

■ *What are our beliefs about communication with regard to who communicates? How much information do they share? How often? Do we solicit input, or just convey information?*

IT is generally not known for its culture of deep sharing. We communicate what people need to do their jobs then we get back to work. I realize I will be communicating much more than is common in our current culture and I also realize that it will be necessary. Often I communicate to my department leads and they communicate with their teams. They share the basic information necessary to do the job, but not much beyond that. Staff meetings are supposed to happen every two weeks, but some groups do not have meetings at all. The informal network has been good enough that we have been able to function, but I realize that is not our "goal state." I also realize that the level of information solicited varies broadly based on who is involved. Some leaders are great at getting input and others would never ask a question if not forced. We may need to have some communication training for our supervisors as part of this process because we have people who are just ill-equipped and terribly uncomfortable communicating an unpopular message to a group. If you add to that discomfort the fact that the team will ask questions and the leader will not have the answer, you could almost guarantee some people will never have a staff meeting until the implementation is done. So, with that in mind we need to get some of these guys, or, even better, everyone into some communication training and I probably need to have a monthly CIO open forum brown bag lunch where everyone is free to come and talk about what is going on. I will have five to ten minutes of prepared information, then, just open dialogue. This will give everyone an opportunity to hear first-hand information as long as they show up, ask, and answer questions.

■ *What type of feedback will we seek from segments to determine if they are buying into the vision (objective and subjective)?*

It looks like the communication lead will be doing some sort of surveys at various intervals to make sure people are moving along the communication curve. He will also get feedback from the sponsors and the extended team. I will have conversations with my team during these lunches and with anyone else who wants to show up as long as we can manage the size. I really want to hear their thoughts and concerns directly, in addition to getting information through surveys. I have no idea if people will show up or not. I really hope they do because the questions they ask will be really helpful for me to get a sense of how well we are doing. I will also count on the communication manager to have a solid handle on what the feedback really means. I understand that people always think they want more information and that sometimes giving too much information too quickly just distracts people from doing their jobs. I will need him to let me know how much is enough based on his experience.

How do we do this?

■ *Do people understand that we need to use the rule of thumb "communicate 7 x 7 or 49" for people to internalize the messages? How do we make this expectation the norm?*

I do not think we understand how much communication is really necessary. I hear from others that it is far more than we can ever imagine and still people seem to not fully understand. The communications manager and I will course correct often. I also think as a steering committee, we will need to be consistent in our message delivery and be clear about our expectation of leaders, sponsors, extended team members, and project team members to actively communicate. We also need to make sure the project team understands that they need to be cautious about what they communicate. They will see all the issues and we want to make sure they convey confidence rather than terror that this may not work. We saw some of this in prior projects—there are some people it may be best to keep out of the communication loop as they are likely to send the wrong message.

■ *Would communication be more effective if multiple projects were discussed in a joint vehicle to help the audience better understand link and impact?*

This idea of communicating multiple projects at the same time seems really important. We have several changes going on at the same time. We need to make sure we are actually coordinating the projects as well as the communications because we could certainly create instability if we change too much without evaluating the impact. Our project communication person has been a manager in the corporate communication office for several years so he understands how to leverage our current communication vehicles as much as possible and will only create separate ones when necessary.

This chapter focused on communicating key messages according to the communication plan to move people from awareness to action and measuring to ensure you are on track. Communication involves multiple groups and the message will be tailored to the audience and delivered through vehicles that make it easy for the recipient. As leaders you will find that you are communicating much more than you anticipated and yet there will still be people who are not as aware as you would expect. It is important to communicate early and often through the entire duration of the project. In the next chapter we will talk about moving from planning to action.

CHAPTER 11

Implement and Measure

Fig. 11.1 Innovative Leadership Development Process

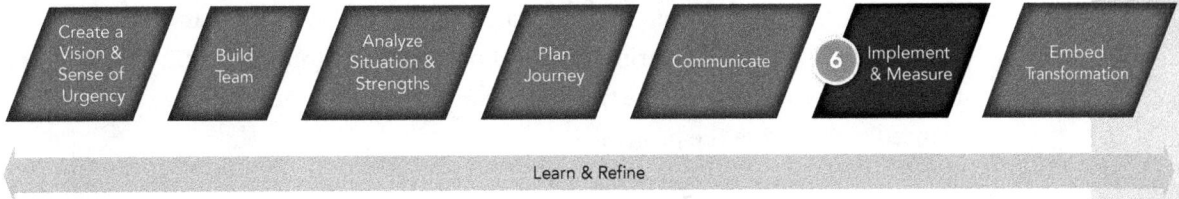

| Create a Vision & Sense of Urgency | Build Team | Analyze Situation & Strengths | Plan Journey | Communicate | 6 Implement & Measure | Embed Transformation |

Learn & Refine

Now that you have built your team, planned your change project, and started communicating, it is time to put your plan into action and measure your progress. Your <u>visible</u> involvement is critical. As you have been completing the reflection questions throughout the process, the section on "what do I do" becomes of the utmost importance in this phase. Are you willing to be visibly engaged in the process? As you return to your plans and charters, you should have a roadmap for your role. As an example, I have included a management activity roadmap in the tools section. Depending on your role within the organization, this type of tool may apply directly to you, or you may rely on other tools such as the leader communication section of the communication strategy discussed in the prior section.

During this phase it is imperative to ensure that your behaviors are aligned with the change you are trying to implement. People will listen to what you say and watch what you do. Additionally, it is important that you are actively involved in communicating, monitoring progress toward implementation through metrics, and delivering appropriate positive reinforcement for success and consequences for groups that are not meeting their commitments.

While this transformation might not be the most pressing activity in your life, for the project team, as they are taking action, it is often the most important professional activity in which they are engaged. Depending on the project pace, they are often exhausted, concerned about project success, engaging in new activities about which they are uncertain, and, in some cases, they hear push back from others in the organization. The project team really benefits from a visible and supportive leader during this phase.

You have put a well-trained project manager in place to run a project. That person will use processes to review risks, issues, results, upcoming milestones, and interdependencies among other topics during the regularly scheduled steering committee meetings and also during regularly scheduled team meetings.

It is important for the project to deliver results quickly to keep people engaged and committed to the vision. You integrated early wins into your plan. It will be important to focus on delivering against those wins and communicating them to key stakeholders while at the same time maintaining focus on the long-term activities required to complete the project.

While the organization is making progress toward the change, it is also actively focused on maintaining momentum for the change effort. It is critical to keep urgency up and minimize the false sense of comfort that may come from early success. It becomes critical to remove all barriers that impede progress, or allow people to continue to do business in ways that conflict with the stated change.

As the project progresses, it will be important to pay attention to morale, ensure the team is managing the stress, and staying actively engaged. If you notice challenges, it will be important to address them actively in a way that is culturally appropriate for your organization. Some organizations hold team building activities and events, and others provide additional support in the way of concierge services. One caution with team building activities: if the team sees these events as yet another activity they are compelled to do that is of little benefit during an already overburdened schedule, it will be counterproductive and you may not accomplish your intended goal of building camaraderie.

The other key focus of this step is measuring progress. Regardless of your project, whether it is a large system change or a smaller pilot, it is important to measure your success against your project goals and also the impact you are having on the overall project goals (when possible). Some projects are structured to implement in small chunks so the impact can be measured at various intervals during implementation. Measures will show if you are on course, and also help you to learn and refine your approach when appropriate.

Tools

Most large projects are managed by a project management office that develops very detailed plans for time phasing of implementation. As a leader, it is important to communicate your primary concerns with regard to how the implementation will begin and ensure that people are not overloaded with activities that will distract them from performing their implementation job well.

During the planning phase, your team likely created a month-by-month Leadership Activity Road Map to summarize leader involvement, and the communication plan specified key leader messages often using tools such as the leader talking points in the prior chapter. The roadmap reflects a leader's monthly activities—what needs to happen month-by-month. In the example below we start with six months prior to project launch or "go live"; however, you will determine the duration of your roadmap based on the complexity of your project. Your role at this point is to make time to take the actions in the plans and work with the team to evaluate the impact you are making—this means things like understanding how communication impacts stakeholders.

Your role as a leader will be to work with the project manager and others to identify gaps that others may have missed, monitor metrics, monitor risk, and provide encouragement for the team. Your project manager will provide the tools for tracking; therefore, we are not providing them in this book. For standard tools, we recommend you refer to the Project Management Institute (www.pmi.org).

Stories and Examples

Now we will return to Paul's ERP implementation. The following Leadership Activity Road Map provides an example of the activity the leaders in Paul's organization will focus on before and during the implementation. It is important to note that as a leader you are taking action during the entire transformation initiative. Each project will have its own tailored activity road map and leader activities will vary broadly depending on the leader-specific role, culture, and project objectives.

This chart is formatted with activities counting back from the date the system is launched (go live) for six months. This timing is captured as T (go live) plus or minus months. It starts with T-6 to denote the activities that will happen six months prior to system launch.

Table 11.1

Vehicle	Month T-6	Month T-5	Month T-4	Month T-3
Leader Activities	▪ Communicate using Project Overview as the foundation for discussions ▪ Monitor and manage risks ▪ Communicate that project will impact everyone in your area ▪ Make the ERP project an agenda item on your monthly meetings ▪ Explain the benefits associated with the project	▪ Communicate using leader talking points ▪ Monitor and manage risks ▪ Explain that job change discussions will take place prior to training ▪ Understand that your direct reports will do their jobs differently ▪ Notify implementation team members of their role and training requirements	▪ Communicate using leader talking points ▪ Monitor and manage risk ▪ Plan work schedules to accommodate training (project management and location steering committee) ▪ Explain the role employees have in the success of the project ▪ Gather questions from employees ▪ Approve training requirements for your end-users ▪ Identify employees who have prerequisite training needs (output of job change workshops [JCW]) ▪ Track implementation team training attendance (Train the Trainer) ▪ Track pre-launch changes and measures	▪ Communicate using leader talking points ▪ Monitor and manage risks ▪ Support the need for data accuracy ▪ Conduct change readiness assessment and take corrective action where necessary ▪ Plan work schedules with training in mind ▪ Reinforce the ERP team on-site support plans with direct report ▪ Approve training requirements for end-users ▪ Plan change discussions ▪ Attend job change integration meetings with cross-functional groups where processes overlap and hand off ▪ Understand process changes in your area ▪ Encourage end-users to use system practice opportunities ▪ Track pre-launch changes and measures

In addition to performing your leadership activities as noted in the Leadership Activity Roadmap, it is important to stay just as actively engaged and fulfilling your roles with the steering committee and project team as you have from the beginning of the project.

Month T-2	Month T-1	Go Live	Month T+1
• Communicate using leader talking points • Understand your own personal behavioral changes and ensure your behavioral change is visible and supportive of the change • Encourage identified end-users to attend training • Explain go live procedures for conversion weekend and following Monday morning • Clearly set expectations for supporting the system • Conduct job change discussions • Track training completion • Change integration workshops may be conducted during this time if better aligned with deployment plan • Measure employee change readiness and take corrective action • Review Day 1 issues and ensure readiness	• Conduct change discussions • Track training completion • Measure change readiness • Review Day 1 issues and ensure readiness		• Track progress and reward performance • Identify corrective action where necessary

Innovative Leadership Reflection Questions

To help you develop your program/project plan, it is time to further clarify your direction, using reflection questions. These questions are organized to reflect the four domains introduced in Section I. As a reminder, this is an opportunity to practice innovative leadership by considering how your change plan will affect changes in your intentions, actions, culture, and systems. These questions are arranged to help you explore each of these domains. The questions for "What do I think/believe?" reflect your intentions. The questions "What do I do?" reflect your actions. The questions "What do we believe?" reflect culture. The questions "How do we do this?" reflect systems. Thus, we designed this exercise to help you start practicing innovative leadership as you create your vision and define your direction.

As a reminder, Table 11.2 contains several questions for each domain to be applicable to a broad range of projects. We recommend you **choose two to four questions** from each domain that best apply to your specific situation.

Table 11.2

QUESTIONS TO GUIDE THE LEADER AND ORGANIZATION

What do I think / believe?

- What do I believe is an effective approach honoring the progress we have made while maintaining focus on the balance of the work that needs to be completed?

- How do I deal with uncertainty and unresolved issues and uncertainty for myself as I lead the change effort forward?

- How do I feel about getting support for my own growth and development during the implementation process?

What do I do?

- How do I publicly recognize people who accomplish wins?

- How does this communication reinforce my own values among the group?

- What changes in my behavior will demonstrate a strong statement to others and support their behavioral and performance changes as well as my own?

- What do I communicate that conveys both progress and continued urgency?

- What am I doing to demonstrate that I "walk the talk"?

- Am I living up to the standards I have set for others?

- Am I perceived as acting with integrity with regard to meeting my commitments?

What do we believe?

- How do we monitor and build morale in different departments as they experience the pressure of balancing daily operations with change?

- What are appropriate rewards in our organization for working on projects, or picking up extra work in the department when key talent is on a project?

- How do we address situations where people or departments actively resist leadership requests to support the change?

- How do different departments (subcultures) maintain morale?

- Do we believe in coaching as to support implementation success?

> **How do we do this?**
>
> - What process do we use to identify barriers to success as we proceed? Do we use a change readiness assessment at multiple times during the process to evaluate changing needs?
>
> - How do we monitor morale during the project to provide an early warning sign for potential risks? What do we do to improve morale?
>
> - How do we minimize blocks that impaired our success in the past? Do we conduct a change history assessment?
>
> - What have we done to identify systems that do not reinforce change and identify tools to resolve issues, such as job starts and stops and mastering new job skills?
>
> - What processes will we establish to identify work that is no longer appropriate or necessary in the changing environment?
>
> - What processes will we create and staff to evaluate the opportunities that can be leveraged to create additional momentum?
>
> - Are we reviewing measures regularly and recognizing results toward the change goals?

Now it is time for Paul to answer the reflection questions. His answers will give insight into the challenges he has faced in past projects and what he will do this time to mitigate some of those issues.

How do I think / believe?

- ***How do I honor the progress we have made while maintaining focus on the balance of the work that needs to be done?***

  As I talk with the team, we will need to celebrate our successes and in my communication, I will be careful to talk about both our success and continued need to maintain momentum. This message will need to become one of my mantras. I assume we will be meeting milestones regularly, and since this is an eighteen-month project we will need to stay focused. I realize that consistently working toward a goal is critical to our success.

- ***How do I deal with and unresolved issues and uncertainty as we move forward?***

  I think one of the more important roles I play as a leader is to set the tone for how we operate. Projects are messy and filled with uncertainty and changes.

While we make every effort to predict and control what happens, it is not realistic to imagine we can predict or control everything. I can be supportive of the fact that we will not know everything, we will be taking calculated risks, we will "conduct experiments," and we will learn as we go. Honestly, this is how I operate best so my contribution to the process will be helping others get comfortable with the uncertainty. I also realize that some people will not want to talk with me about their concerns. I have always been a fan of coaching during these times. I work with a coach and encourage others to do the same.

What do I do?

■ *How do I publicly recognize people who accomplish the wins?*

Public communication is tricky. It seems that some people do not like public recognition and others get frustrated if they believe they worked as hard as the person getting the recognition. I tend to prefer personal and private recognition. I will stop by and thank people for contributing and also give a token of our appreciation like a gift card for an evening out. The safest approach is to confine public recognition to the project team meetings and also in the project newsletter. Fortunately, as a company we already have a nice appreciation system so I can just leverage that rather than creating something special. The company gives "Bravo" awards to employees who make a significant contribution and allows us to give gift cards. The system addresses all of the tax implications. I leverage systems that are already in place whenever possible. It is unfortunate to try something simple like giving a gift card only to realize that I have negatively impacted someone's pay because this is actually taxable income.

■ *How does this communication reinforce my own values among the group?*

I addressed this topic in a prior question: we will be facing ongoing change and uncertainty. I can set the tone through the timbre of my voice and my conversations with people throughout the organization. I will reinforce my expectations that things will change, things will go wrong, we will have issues—and all of that is just a normal part of the process. I will try to remain calm as we talk about changes and uncertainty. Many of my actions reinforce my belief that creating a culture of safety is critical to implementation success. I can talk about the idea of shifting from a "predict and control" model into an approach that integrates experimentation as part of the way we get things done. This shift will require ongoing reinforcement, and is an important shift for the steering committee and the project team to make. I am now using new behaviors and experimenting with new leadership skills, and it is important for me to be mindful of my own words and how they align with my behaviors.

What do we believe?

■ *What are appropriate rewards in our organization for working on projects? For picking up extra work in the department when key talent is on a project?*

We have not really resolved the question of rewards. We are asking team members to work outside of their comfort zone designing something new. We expect them to work consistently long hours and many of them are traveling. We are researching a concierge service to help them take care of the things they would do if they were at home. If we pay a bonus that approximates what they are paying for extra support and inconvenience, that seems reasonable. For those who are living in an apartment and not incurring extra costs, this will be a windfall. For others, they are hiring people to accomplish tasks they would be doing if they were home and working normal hours.

The issue of people staying in their home departments picking up extra work is a harder one. We recognize everyone will be working more during this project and, realistically, that is just part of the ebb and flow of business. In this time of rapid change, while I realize there is inconvenience for everyone, if we do not all pitch in and ensure we are staying current, employees will have the much bigger challenge of unemployment. We need our department managers to stay on top and make reasonable demands. If not, we will authorize additional funding for either overtime or additional staffing.

■ *How do we address situations where people or departments actively resist leadership requests to support the change?*

We have given a great deal of autonomy to general managers because we trust they know how to run their businesses. This is touchy because we are now stepping in and telling them to do something they may not agree with. The process is easier when they agree. Part of my job as a leader is to try to understand their concerns and resistance, and help to address it. In some cases their concerns are valid and we missed something in our planning that is unique to them. I know we need to stay open minded to their concerns. This takes a lot of patience when I have other priorities that I need to attend to. I also understand it is necessary. There does come a point where the listening and negotiation end, and I will simply give a directive. As an organization, the senior leadership team decided to make this investment and we need to implement it across the entire enterprise. I hope we are able to get everyone on board, but, if we can't, we will need to deal with the consequences.

How do we do this?

■ *As we proceed, what process do we use to identify barriers to success? Do we use a change readiness assessment at multiple times during the process to evaluate changing needs?*

We have a very experienced project manager who will maintain an ongoing issues log and risk log. Each project team will give input to these logs.

In addition to monitoring issues and risks, it is important to proactively manage the systems and processes that impact performance. It is generally change management and coaching teams that monitor the human change elements, including administering change readiness surveys and communication impact surveys. They are shooting for specific targets and if the organization is falling short of the targets, they will identify the cause and work to address it, either through the issues and risks log, or through specific processes designed to support behavioral and performance change. This team is also proactively anticipating barriers and risks. They are tracking the possible Day 1 issues and the "Top 10 Must Do Activities" to ensure go live will be successful.

■ *How do we minimize blocks that impaired our success in the past? Do we conduct a change history assessment?*

During the assessment phase, we conducted a change history assessment and identified what worked well and what did not work in past projects. Fortunately, our project manager was involved in several other projects internally and before working for us, she worked for a large consulting firm, so she has great experience with other organizations. As I mentioned in the prior question, we are tracking the possible Day 1 issues and the "Top 10 Must Do Activities" to ensure go live will be successful. These two items were initiated in part as a response to prior challenges. By implementing this process, we are being very proactive in anticipating what could go wrong (based on history and experiences of other organizations) and building a plan to mitigate risk.

This chapter focused on taking action—doing the activities we defined during the planning phase. This is where much of the work is actually accomplished and the role of the leader becomes staying involved in the monitoring and measuring as well as communicating, rewarding, and measuring morale. This phase of the project can last for months, and in some cases years. It is important as a leader that you make sure you maintain your focus as you get pulled off to other pressing priorities. In the next chapter we will talk about moving from action to embedding the changes systemically.

CHAPTER 12
Embed Transformation Systematically

Figure 12.1 Innovative Leadership Development Process

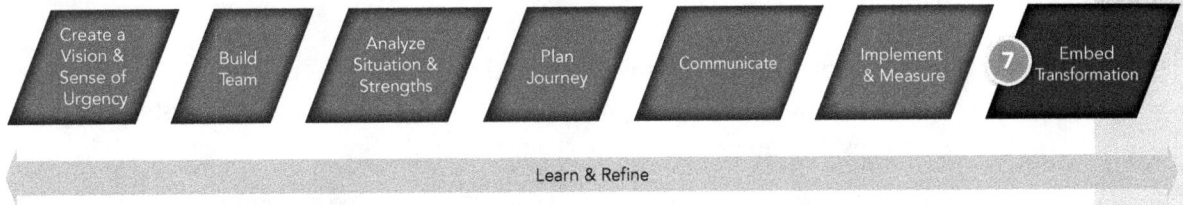

Create a Vision & Sense of Urgency → Build Team → Analyze Situation & Strengths → Plan Journey → Communicate → Implement & Measure → 7 Embed Transformation

Learn & Refine

This stage is when the organization solidifies the change and it becomes part of normal life rather than a special project. Some of the actions that can encourage the change to take root include: updating the recruiting and on-boarding processes, refining the promotion process to reward those who behave in accordance with the stated goals, and creating new stories that reinforce the new culture.

To maintain momentum, it is critical to retain a sense of urgency while minimizing the sense of comfort that may come from early success. Be aware that it is easy to stray from your goals if you declare success based on your early results, especially when other projects tug at your time and attention. One helpful shift in thinking is to see the actions you are taking as a practice. You are practicing your disciplined business activities in the same fashion that a professional athlete practices a particular sport. The most successful athletes are constantly practicing to improve, even though they may already be the best in the world. You will need to consider making time in the long term for activities that best foster success and help maintain your support system.

Therefore, ask yourself: "When I see progress, what will keep me using the disciplined practices and business processes that made me successful? How do I ensure they are sustained? I need some reminder that my progress is a result of engaged practice, and my performance is likely to suffer if I do not maintain a proper focus." These changes include both my personal changes as a leader and the changes the organization is making.

Additionally, by this point, you may want to re-evaluate your goals and begin raising the bar. You will need to balance establishing a long-term discipline to sustain progress while identifying your next strategic initiatives and goals.

Tools

Below is a table you can use to capture and track processes that are impacted by the change and actions that need to take place to ensure that the overall system supports the changes. Examples of systemic changes include:

- Update new employee orientation – identify outdated content and update
- Update training – someone will inventory which training modules teach the processes that will be replaced
- Update job descriptions for roles that change
- Review/update compensation for roles that change
- Review compensation approach – is the current structure consistent with the changes we are making and does the system incentivize the behaviors we expect?

Use the following worksheet to help you document the processes that need to be changed to fully realize the value of the projects you are completing.

Table 12.1

PROCESSES IMPACTING SUSTAINABILITY

Impacted processes	Recommended action	Expected impact	By when	Measure	Status	Process owner
Top 1	1.					
	2.					
	3.					
Top 2	4.					
	5.					
	6.					
Top 3	7.					
	8.					
	9.					

Organization Transformation Reflection Questions

To help you develop your action plan, it is time to further clarify your direction, using reflection questions. These questions are organized to reflect the four domains introduced in Section I. As a reminder, this is an opportunity to practice innovative leadership by considering how your change plan will affect changes in your intentions, actions, culture, and systems. These questions are arranged to help you explore each of these domains. The questions for "What do I think/believe?" reflect your intentions. The questions "What do I do?" reflect your actions. The questions "What do we believe?" reflect culture. The questions "How do we do this?" reflect systems. Thus, we designed this exercise to help you start practicing innovative leadership as you create your vision and define your direction.

As a reminder, the table contains several questions for each domain to be applicable to a broad range of projects. We recommend you **choose two to four questions** from each domain that best apply to your specific situation.

Table 12.2

QUESTIONS TO GUIDE THE LEADER AND ORGANIZATION
What do I think / believe?
▪ What progress have I made as a leader, as a person?
▪ Am I still in the right role for my personal values and mission?
▪ When I think of my mental, emotional, moral, and physical state, am I still the right person for the job ahead?
What do I do?
▪ What do I do that reinforces the value of the change to individuals and to the organization?
▪ What do I do to encourage people to continue the behavioral changes they made during the project?
▪ How do I continue to show the new behaviors I have publicly and privately committed to?
▪ How do I emphasize the focus on systematic change that encourages, but does not insist, on personal growth?

What do we believe?

- How do we see ourselves now?
- How will organizational goals and values change based on the change effort?
- How do we react to old behaviors that no longer support the organization?
- How do we shift our focus in support of long change efforts without losing the value of recent gains?
- How do we honor our past while also making these changes?
- How do we incorporate new jargon, best practices, and human interest into emerging organizational stories?
- How do our rewards for small accomplishments push us toward the overall organizational success?

How do we do this?

- How does the organization acknowledge people who have made the desired changes (job starts and stops) and mastered new skills?
- Do we continue to measure and reward actions necessary to sustain the change using the updated job descriptions and process metrics developed during the project?
- How does the organization fund, staff, and supply sufficient and appropriate infrastructure to support and reinforce new behaviors and culture? (These may include promotions, orientation, rewards, and recognition.)
- Have we built the changes into the ongoing training processes?
- Have we sufficiently updated employee orientation and other human resources and IT systems to support changes in goals and values?
- How have we incorporated the "Top 10 list" into our systems and processes?
- Have we reviewed objective and subjective measures regularly and recognized results that impact the change goals?
- Are we reinforcing actions that positively influence the larger vision and examining those that do not?
- Have we developed and tracked success measures and created feedback and improvement loops?
- Are we making changes based on feedback?

Now it is time for Paul to answer the reflection questions. His answers will give insight into the challenges he has faced in past projects and what he will do this time to mitigate some of those issues.

What do I think / believe?

■ *What progress have I made as a leader, as a person?*

I developed myself as a leader throughout this large project. I have a much better understanding of myself and my personal leadership strengths and preferences. I also have a clearer understanding of my limitations and where I need to work with others to drive successful organizational change.

I have a much stronger sense of how the overall enterprise operates with all of the intricacies and nuances—something I did not understand before. I also better understand the cultures of the different offices domestically and abroad. This stronger understanding positions me to make an even stronger impact on the organization than I did when I joined the company.

■ *Am I still in the right role for my personal values and mission?*

As I learn more about the company, I have developed an even higher regard for individuals and the overall company. This is a company I feel good about working for and I want to build on the success we created during this project. I'm excited about our successes and the prospects for my future and our company's future.

■ *When I think of my mental, emotional, moral, and physical state, am I still the right person for the job ahead?*

This project was both exhausting and exhilarating. I do need to take some time off and also cut my hours to something that will allow me to spend more time with my family. It is interesting that while I was working really long hours, I focused on my health more than I have during times with less pressure. I want to maintain the progress I made in building some good habits during this stressful project.

What do I do?

■ *What do I do that reinforces the value of the change to individuals and to the organization?*

During the project we changed the performance management system for key roles within the organization. I need to be sure that we are using this new system on an ongoing basis and really rewarding the people who played key roles. I also want to make sure I personally acknowledge people who are leading the change with regard to adopting the new processes—publicly and privately as I find opportunities.

On the organizational side, it will be important to continue to look for ways to reinforce our changes and identify barriers that will arise over time to the new way of doing business. It is interesting how persistent habits are and how easy it is to fall back into old patterns. Our best leaders find themselves doing this and we need to identify and address it in an open and supportive way among the leadership team.

■ *How do I emphasize the focus on systematic change that encourages, but does not insist, on personal growth?*

There is no question that we are making and focusing on systematic change. We have implemented a new system and new processes and many people are still uncomfortable with these changes. As a company, we expect people to make the changes necessary to perform their immediate jobs. There is no requirement to develop further; however, people who continue to grow and develop proactively generally perform better in the long term. While this is my preference, we do not require growth beyond the ability to perform the job.

What do we believe?

■ *How do we see ourselves now?*

We used to see ourselves as good people working hard. We did not rely heavily on formal processes or measures. People know their jobs, and as long as we did not experience significant change, we were able to perform very effectively. We have now shifted to a culture that values a more formally structured approach to designing and performing work. We all have detailed job descriptions as a result of this process. We are measured against our results and that is how we are rewarded. It is different than what people were accustomed to, but they seem to be adapting. Some really like the new approach and are starting friendly competitions to see who can deliver the best results in the department. That competition is new behavior and as long as people are still willing to pitch in and help one another, a bit more competition seems healthy.

■ *How do we honor our past while also making these changes?*

Our organization has a very proud legacy and I do want to confirm that people understand we are adapting to the times while honoring what got us here. Our history distinguishes us from many of our competitors and is something we need to retain—which seems odd since we are changing so much. We need to be clear about which elements of our culture are not to be changed and which elements need to be updated to keep pace with the times. This is a tricky balance. If we hold too much to the past, we will lose our competitive advantage and could even risk going out of business. Yet, if we change too much, we lose the very characteristics that make us unique. While there are no easy answers, we, as a leadership team, are responsible for setting the guidelines. Given that responsibility, we are a really strong team, I am confident we will make good decisions as a group about what to retain and what to change.

How do we do this?

■ *How does the organization acknowledge people who have made the desired changes (job starts and stops) and mastered new skills?*

Many folks on the project team were identified for the newly created roles that support the system. Most of these people are in roles of higher responsibility with higher pay. Promotion, satisfying work, and a pay increase are certainly nice rewards for dedication to the project. We have also identified high-potential people given their dedication to mastering the new skills and their involvement in the project who may be included in our next round of training.

For people who have done an exceptional job in developing new skills but either did not get new roles or were not involved in the project implementation, we have an existing performance management and bonus system that varies by level within the organization. This system was designed to give visible and financial rewards for accomplishments. We are using that to acknowledge many people. We found that it is better to work within existing reward systems when at all possible rather than spending additional time and energy creating one-off systems. Rewards can range from a small token of appreciation like a company logo shirt to a significant bonus. We are trying to be sure that the reward is commensurate to the accomplishment.

■ *Have we built the changes into the ongoing training processes?*

One thing I found amazing is how broadly this change has made an impact on the organization. We need to make a significant investment in training because the changes were so pervasive company-wide within the system, processes, culture, and all of the supporting systems, such as performance appraisals and the performance management system company-wide. We will take this opportunity to update our training approach in many cases. We need to be able to make changes to our training going forward using a more agile approach. We expect changes to accelerate and if training is customized for each location, the time and investment in training is out of balance with what is necessary. We continue to find processes and delivery mechanisms that must be updated. Some of these changes are necessary because of our ERP project. Others just become obvious because we realize that what we were doing is outdated and this is a good time to make additional changes.

Celebrate your success

What's next for you?

Through this book, we've provided a framework for innovative leadership and a process to transform your organization. We augmented the process with a series of practical questions and templates that can serve as guides. Based on our work with several hundred clients over the last twelve years, we offer this specific combination of tools and frameworks to create a comprehensive framework and practical tools that will allow you, the leader, and your team to understand the innovative leadership framework and use it along with the transformation process to transform your organization.

Additionally, we provided the story of Paul to illustrate how to use the transformation process. He uses the tools in the book and answers the questions to illustrate how a Strategist level leader would transform his organization. It is through Paul's explorations that we share the practical application of this theory with you.

Now that you have completed the first round of the guide and you have established a solid understanding of innovative leadership and will have successfully implemented an organizational change, it is time to think about whether you want to enhance your practice and begin the process again. Do you want to build on what you have created with the *Innovative Leadership Fieldbook,* or this guide, or revisit parts of that may be valuable at this time? You could start from the beginning with another organizational goal, or start with yourself and examine how to further develop your leadership based on this project. Future iterations will likely take less time as you now have experience with the process. You may find that you focus in different areas based on your personal or organizational growth.

APPENDIX
Additional Worksheets

These additional blank worksheets are duplicates of several tables found within the guide to allow you to capture your notes.

Table 1.4 – Page 44

ENNEAGRAM QUICK REFERENCE

TYPE	Name	Characteristics	Your Score	Your Notes
One	Reformer	Rational, principled, self-controlled		
Two	Helper	Caring, generous, possessive		
Three	Achiever	Adaptable, ambitious, image-conscious		
Four	Individualist	Intuitive, aesthetic, self-absorbed		
Five	Investigator	Perceptive, innovative, detached		
Six	Loyalist	Engaging, responsible, defensive		
Seven	Enthusiast	Upbeat, accomplished, impulsive		
Eight	Challenger	Self-confident, decisive, domineering		
Nine	Peacemaker	Receptive, reassuring, complacent		
TOTAL:			100%	

Table 2.4 – Page 61

DEVELOPMENTAL PERSPECTIVE QUICK REFERENCE

Description of Developmental Levels / Perspectives	Your Score	Your Notes
Diplomat ■ Demonstrates predominately concrete thinking style ■ Hyper-concerned with social acceptance ■ Emphasis on conforming to the rules and norms of the desired group ■ Imagines that others think and feel the same as they do		
Expert ■ Demonstrates basic abstract thinking ■ Concerned with expressing a sense of individuality in sharp contrast to others ■ Concerned with measuring up to the "right" standards ■ Can often appear to be a perfectionist ■ Makes constant comparisons with others to gauge identity ■ Can often be critical and blame-oriented ■ Adept at developing multiple new solutions to problems but not able to determine the best fit solution ■ Can begin envisioning short-term time horizons: three months to one year		

Table 2.4 Continued

Description of Developmental Levels / Perspectives	Your Score	Your Notes
Achiever ■ Basic ability to identify shades of grey and see conceptual complexity ■ Focuses on causes, achievement, and effectiveness ■ Considers others while pursuing their own individual agendas and ideas ■ Sees themselves as part of the larger group, yet separate and responsible for their own choices ■ Appreciates mutual expression of differences ■ Time horizon: one to five-years		
Individualist ■ Increased capacity for advanced complex thinking ■ Exhibits an ability to appreciate paradox in circumstances ■ Begins to value and use rudimentary aspects of intuition ■ Beginning awareness that perception shapes reality, including their own ■ Self-reflective and investigative of their own personalized assumptions, as well as those of others ■ Understands mutual interdependence with others ■ Lives personal convictions according to internal standards ■ Interest in feedback becomes very important ■ Longer time horizon: five to ten years ■ Tend to move into change agent/consultant/portfolio roles		

Table 2.4 Continued

Description of Developmental Levels / Perspectives	Your Score	Your Notes
Strategist ▪ Perceives systematic patterns and long-term trends with uncanny clarity ▪ Can easily differentiate objective versus subjective biased events ▪ Exhibits a strong focus on self-development, self-actualization, and authenticity ▪ Pursues actualizing personal convictions according to internal standards ▪ Management style is tenacious, yet humble ▪ Understands the importance of mutual interdependence with others ▪ Integrating feedback into performance is very important ▪ Tend to move into change agent/consultant/portfolio roles ▪ Well-advanced time horizon: approximately fifteen to twenty years with concern for legacy		
Magician / Alchemist ▪ Seeks transformation of organizations not according to conventional goals but according to a higher order ▪ Has a transforming ability to draw together opposites and initiate new directions from creative tension ▪ Tends to build their own novel organizations or work on their own to offer their best contribution to humanity ▪ Seen as visionary leaders ▪ May lead from behind, or in a more subtle way ▪ Time horizon: in excess of twenty years		
TOTAL:	100%	

Table 3.3 – Page 81

RESILIENCE QUICK REFERENCE

Keys to Building & Retaining Personal Resilience	Your Score	Your Notes
Manage Thinking Practice telling yourself: - Challenges are normal and healthy for any individual or organization - My current problem is a doorway to an innovative solution - I feel inspired about the opportunity to create new possibilities that did not exist before		
Maintain Physical Well-Being Are you getting enough: - Sleep - Exercise - Healthy food - Time in nature - Time to meditate and relax Are you limiting or eliminating: - Caffeine - Nicotine		

Table 3.3 Continued

Keys to Building & Retaining Personal Resilience	Your Score	Your Notes
Using Emotional Intelligence to Fulfill Life Purpose Understand what you stand for. Maintain focus. Ask: ■ What is my purpose? ■ Why is it important to me? ■ What values do I hold that will enable me to accomplish my purpose? ■ What opportunities in my professional life help me to achieve my life purpose?		
Harness the Power of Connection Practice effective communication: ■ Say things simply and clearly ■ Make communication safe by being responsive ■ Encourage people to ask questions and clarify if they do not understand your message ■ Balance advocacy for your point with inquiring about the other person's points ■ When you have a different point of view, seek to understand how and why the other person believes what they do in a non-threatening way ■ When in doubt, share information and emotions ■ Build trust by acting for the greater good		
TOTAL:		

243

Table 5.2 – Page 104

LEADERSHIP BEHAVIORS QUICK REFERENCE

LCP Dimension Definitions		Your Notes
Creative Leadership Behaviors reflect key behaviors and internal assumptions that lead to high fulfillment, high achievement leadership.		
The **Relating** Dimension measures a leader's capability to relate to others in a way that brings out the best in people, groups and organizations. It comprises: - Caring Connection - Fosters Team Play - Collaborator - Mentoring and Developing - Interpersonal Intelligence		
The **Self-Awareness** Dimension measures the leader's orientation to ongoing professional and personal development, as well as the degree to which inner self-awareness is expressed through high integrity leadership. It comprises: - Selfless Leader - Balance - Composure - Personal Learner		
The **Authenticity** Dimension measures the leader's capability to relate to others in an authentic, courageous, and high integrity manner. It comprises: - Integrity - Authenticity		

Table 5.2 Continued

LCP Dimension Definitions	Your Notes
The **Systems Awareness** Dimension measures the degree to which the leader's awareness is focused on whole system improvement and on community welfare (the symbiotic relationship between the long-term welfare of the community and the interests of the organization). It comprises: ■ Community Concern ■ Sustainable Productivity ■ Systems Thinker	
The **Achieving** Dimension measures the extent to which the leader offers visionary, authentic, and high accomplishment leadership. It comprises: ■ Strategic Focus ■ Purposeful and Visionary ■ Achieves Results ■ Decisiveness	
Reactive Leadership Styles reflect inner beliefs that limit effectiveness, authentic expression, and empowering leadership.	
The **Controlling** Dimension measures the extent to which the leader establishes a sense of personal worth through task accomplishment and personal achievement. Dimensions include: ■ Perfect ■ Driven ■ Ambition ■ Autocratic	

Table 5.2 Continued

LCP Dimension Definitions	Your Score	Your Notes
The **Protecting** Dimension which measures the belief that the leader can feel safe and establish a sense of worth through withdrawal, remaining distant, hidden, aloof, cynical, superior, and/or rational. Dimensions include: ■ Arrogance ■ Critical ■ Distance		
The **Complying** Dimension measures the extent to which the leader gets a sense of self-worth and security by following the direction of others rather than acting on his own intentions and wants. Dimensions include: ■ Conservative ■ Pleasing ■ Belonging ■ Passive		
TOTAL:	100%	

Table 6.1 – Page 111

CHANGE FOUNDATION ASSESSMENT – Key Components

Data source:											
Organizational vision:											
Strategic goal:											
Project objectives:											
Key stakeholders:											
Diagnostic activities:											
Expected changes:											
Approval:											
Project motivation:											
Implementation activities:											
Processes in scope:											
Resources:											

Table 6.2 – Page 113

SAMPLE PROJECT CHARTER – Key Components

1. Business problem statement:	
2. Project focus:	
3. Project vision and objectives:	
4. Project guiding principles:	
5. Risk of not implementing project:	
6. Project sponsors, steering committee, key project team members:	
7. Individual and team learning objectives:	
8. High level scope:	
9. High level deliverables:	
10. Project assumptions and constraints:	
11. High level schedule:	
12. Interconnected projects:	
13. Charter approval signatures:	

Table 7.1 – Page 142

TEAM SELECTION MATRIX

Criteria	Functional Expertise Y/N	Communication Y/N	Teamwork Y/N	Credibility Y/N	Trust Y/N	Culture Y/N	Commitment Y/N	Developmental Perspective (Level)	Commitment to Develop Y/N
Steering Committee									
Chair									
Member									
Member									
Member									
Sponsors									
Project Team Members									
Project Manager									
Team Lead									
Member									
Member									
Member									

Table 7.2 – Page 143

TEAM CHARTER

Team objectives:	
Team learning objectives:	
Major deliverables:	
Responsibilities:	
Engagement:	
Timing:	
Measure of success:	
Resource requirements:	

Table 8.3 – Page 165

STAKEHOLDER IMPACT ANALYSIS

Stakeholder name (Group)	Who to interview	Impact of change	Perception of change	Role supporting change	Level of commitment (h, m, l)

Table 8.4 – Page 166

USER IMPACT ANALYSIS

Function / process	Process / people changes	New skills	Position changes

Table 8.5 – Page 167

CHANGE INITIATIVE INVENTORY

Change initiative	Description	Who impacted (user groups / plants)	How does it impact project?	Project timing

Table 9.2 – Page 184

LEADER DEVELOPMENT WORKSHEET – Evaluate and Select Behavioral Change Priorities

Key Actions	Detailed Action Planning	Skill 1	Skill 2
Select Behaviors	Which behaviors do I want to improve or change? Which behaviors do I perform well that I would like to enhance?		
What are the consequences of this behavior?	What will happen if I continue to demonstrate this behavior in the future? How does this behavior impact my customers? How does it impact my career? How are my colleagues impacted? How is my organization impacted?		
Why do I demonstrate this behavior?	I have developed behaviors over the course of my life because they make sense. What has changed that now makes this behavior ineffective?		
How would I like to perform in the future?	Write an end-result statement describing the changes I will make and the impact of those changes. What will an observer see when I have made this change?		
Who will help me change?	Who could I ask to provide me with feedback on how I am doing? Who would be a good mentor?		
What type of support do I want?	Make an agreement with a person you trust about how you would like to support one another in changing behaviors. How will that person hold me accountable for taking this step? How will I support them in changing their behavior? Is there a group that will support me long term?		
What will I do or not do?	What other actions could I take? What am I willing to commit to doing? What am I committed to stopping?		
When will I complete actions?	When will I have completed action items?		

Table 9.3 – Page 186

DEVELOPMENT PLANNING WORKSHEET

Current State	Future State / Goal	Actions	By When?	Measure - How do you know?

Table 12.1 – Page 228

PROCESSES IMPACTING SUSTAINABILITY

Impacted processes	Recommended action	Expected impact	By when	Measure	Status	Process owner
Top 1	1.					
	2.					
	3.					
Top 2	4.					
	5.					
	6.					
Top 3	7.					
	8.					
	9.					

Resources

This section includes additional recommendations to augment the fieldbook for those who want more in-depth information.

Resources Chapter 1

One of the most powerful tools for understanding ourselves is the Enneagram, an ancient symbol of unity and diversity, change and transformation. There are several very solid enneagram resources. The one we use most often for leadership groups is: www.enneagraminstitute.com

www.enneagraminstitute.com

Resources Chapter 2

The theoretical research of Susann Cook-Greuter and Terri O'Fallon provide the most recent and complete references available in support of Developmental levels and their applications. Both can be found on their websites.

www.cook-greuter.com
www.pacificintegral.com

Cindy Wigglesworth provides a spiritual intelligence competency model designed to improve leadership effectiveness.

www.deepchange.com

Resources Chapter 4

Ken Wilber is the original philosopher and founder of Integral Theory. He has written over 30 books on the subject. He founded the Integral Institute whose mission is: to awaken humanity to full self-awareness. By providing research, education and events that foster intentional, behavioral, cultural and social self-awareness, the Institute helps global leaders from all arenas to improve the human condition. The Institute's vision is that humanity lives with the awareness necessary to compassionately integrate the fragmented and partial perspectives of differing pursuits of the good life.

The Institute aims to help solve the world's most complex problems. Among the primary goals of the Institute are research and cultivation of leadership of complex, global issues facing humanity in the 21st century, and in particular, those issues that can only be solved with a comprehensive, Integral and non-partial approach to the complex interdependencies that tend to characterize these issues. Global warming; evolutionary forms of capitalism; and the culture wars in political, religious, and scientific domains are all examples of problems to which the Institute hopes to bring new clarity.

www.integralinstitute.org

Resources Chapter 5

For more information about The Leadership Circle Profile or to have assessments conducted see the study written by Bob Anderson and published by *The Leadership Circle, The Leadership Circle and Organizational Performance, 2007.*

www.theleadershipcircle.com

References

Brown, Barrett. "Conscious Leadership for Sustainability: How Leaders with Late-Stage Action Logic Design and Engage in Sustainability Initiatives." Ph.D. diss., Fielding Graduate University, 2011.

Collins, Jim. *Good to Great: Why some Companies Make the Leap… and Others Don't*. New York: HarperCollins Publishers, Inc., 2001.

Cook-Greuter, Susanne. "A Detailed Description of Nine Action Logics in the Leadership Development Framework Adapted from Leadership Development Theory," www.cook-greuter.com. 2002.

Csikszentmihalyi, Mihaly. *Flow: The Psychology of Optimal Experience*. New York: Harper Perennial, 1990.

Fitch, Geoff, Venita Ramirez, and Terri O'Fallon. "Enacting Containers for Integral Transformative Development." Presentation: Integral Theory Conference, July 2010.

Gauthier, Alain. "Developing Generative Change Leaders Across Sectors: An Exploration of Integral Approaches," *Integral Leadership Review*, June 2008.

Daniel Goleman. *Emotional Intelligence*. New York: Bantam Books, 1995.

Goleman, Daniel, Richard E. Boyatzis, and Annie McKee. *Primal Leadership: Learning to Lead with Emotional Intelligence*. Boston: Harvard Business School Press, 2002.

Goleman, Daniel. *Working with Emotional Intelligence*. New York: Bantam Books, 1998.

Heath, Chip and Dan Heath. *Switch: How to Change Things When Change Is Hard*. New York: Broadway Books, 2010.

Ronald A. Heifetz and Donald A. Laurie. "The Work of Leadership." *Harvard Business Review on Breakthrough Leadership*, December 2001.

Heifetz, Ronald A., Grashow, Alexander, Linsky, Marty. *The Practice of Adaptive Leadership: Tools and Tactics for Changing Your Organization and the World*. Cambridge Leadership Associates, 2009.

Howe-Murphy, Roxanne. *Deep Coaching: Using the Enneagram as a Catalyst for Profound Change*. El Granada: Enneagram Press, 2007

Isern, Joseph, Meaney, Mary C., Wilson, Sarah. "Corporate Transformation under Pressure." McKinsey & Company, 2009.

Klatt, Maryanna, Janet Buckworth, and William B. Malarkey. "Effects of Low-Dose Mindfulness-Based Stress Reduction (MBSR-ld) on Working Adults." Health Education and Behavior. Vol. 36, no. 3. 2009: 601-614.

John P. Kotter, "Accelerate!" *Harvard Business Review*, November 2012.

Loehr, Jim & Schwartz, Tony. "The Power of Full Engagement: Managing Energy, Not Time, Is the Key to High Performance and Personal Renewal." Free Press Publications.

Loehr, Jim, Tony Schwartz. "The Making of a Corporate Athlete." *Harvard Business Review*. 2001

Maddi, Salvatore R. and Deborah M. Khoshaba. *Resilience at Work: How to Succeed No Matter What Life Throws at You.* New York: MJF Books, 2005.

Metcalf, Maureen. "Level 5 Leadership: Leadership that Transforms Organizations and Creates Sustainable Results." *Integral Leadership Review*. March 2008.

Metcalf, Maureen, John Forman, and Dena Paluck. "Implementing Sustainable Transformation – Theory and Application." *Integral Leadership Review*. June 2008.

Metcalf, Maureen and Dena Paluck. "The Story of Jill–How an Individual Leader Developed into a 'Level 5' Leader." *Integral Leadership Review*. June 2010.

Northouse, Peter G. *Leadership: Theory and Practice.* Thousand Oaks: Sage Publications, 2010.

O'Fallon, Terri, Venita Ramirez, Jesse McKay, and Kari Mays. "Collective Individualism: Experiments in Second Tier Community." Presented August, 2008 at the Integral Theory Conference.

O'Fallon, Terri. "The Collapse of the Wilber-Combs Matrix: The Interpenetration of the State and Structure Stages." Presented July, 2010 at the Integral Theory Conference (1st place winner).

O'Fallon, Terri. "Integral Leadership Development: Overview of our Leadership Development Approach." www.pacificintegral.com, 2011.

Richmer, Hilke R. An Analysis of the Effects of Enneagram-Based Leader Development On Self-Awareness: A Case Study At A Midwest Utility Company. Ph.D. diss., Spalding University, 2011.

Riso, Don Richard, and Russ Hudson. The Wisdom of the Enneagram: *The Complete Guide to Psychological and Spiritual Growth for the Nine Personality Types.* New York: Bantam, 1999.

Riso, Don Richard, and Russ Hudson. *Personality Types: Using the Enneagram for Self-Discovery.* New York: Houghton Mifflin, 1996.

Rooke, David and William R. Torbert. "Seven Transformations of Leadership, Leaders are made, not born, and how they develop is critical for organizational change," *Harvard Business Review*, April 2005.

Rooke, David and William R. Torbert. "Organizational Transformation as a Function of CEOs' Developmental Stage." *Organization Development Journal* 16, 1, 1998: 11-28.

Senge, Peter, Art Kleiner, Charlotte Roberts, Richard Ross, and Bryan Smith. *The Fifth Discipline Fieldbook: Strategies and Tools for Building a Learning Organization.* New York: Doubleday, 1994.

Senge, Peter, Art Kleiner, Charlotte Roberts, George Roth, Richard Ross, and Bryan Smith. The Dance of Change: *The Challenges to Sustaining Momentum in Learning Organizations.* New York: Random House, 1999.

Strebel, "Why Do Employees Resist Change?" *Harvard Business Review*, February 2000.

Torbert, William R. and Associates. *Action Inquiry: The Secret of Timely and Transforming Leadership.* San Francisco: Berrett-Koehler Publishing, Inc. 2004.

Wigglesworth, Cindy. "Why Spiritual Intelligence Is Essential to Mature Leadership," *Integral Leadership Review* August, 2006.

"Introduction to Integral Theory and Practice: IOS Basic and AQAL Map." www.integralnaked.org. 2003.

Wilber, Ken, Terry Patten, Adam Leonard and Marco Morelli. *Integral Life Practice: A 21st-Century Blueprint for Physical Health, Emotional Balance, Mental Clarity, and Spiritual Awakening.* Integral Books, 2008.

About the Author

Maureen Metcalf

Maureen Metcalf is the Founder and CEO of Metcalf & Associates, Inc., a management consulting and coaching firm dedicated to helping leaders, their management teams and organizations implement the innovative leadership practices necessary to thrive in a rapidly changing environment.

Maureen is an acclaimed thought leader who developed, tested, and implemented emerging models that dramatically improve leaders and organizations success in changing times. She works with leaders to develop innovative leadership capacity and with organizations to further develop innovative leadership qualities. Maureen is on the forefront of helping organizations to explore these emerging solutions for long term organizational sustainability.

As a senior manager with two "Big Four" Management consulting firms for 12 years, Maureen managed and contributed to the successful completion of a wide array of projects from strategy development and organizational design for start-up companies to large system change for well-established organizations. She has worked with a number of Fortune 100 clients delivering a wide range of significant business results such as: increased profitability, cycle time reduction, increased employee engagement and effectiveness, and improved quality.

www.ingramcontent.com/pod-product-compliance
Lightning Source LLC
Chambersburg PA
CBHW061808210326
41599CB00034B/6925